Scotland's Wild Salmon:
Surviving in a Changing World?

Drew Jamieson

By the same Author

The Ochil Hills: A Special Place (2018)
Where the Wild Trout Swim (2018)
Where the Wild Salmon Run, (2018)
A Scottish Angler's Companions (2018)
Trout from Scottish Reservoirs (2019)
The Trout Reservoirs of Lothian (2019)

Independently published
Available on Amazon

Front Cover: "Salmon 'Loup' "
Reproduced by kind permission of The Estate of
Colin Gibson.

Title Page: "Leaping Salmon"
Reproduced by kind permission of The Estate of C.F. Tunnicliffe
OBE, RA.

Dedication

To Morny, my wife and lifelong "angler's companion",
through the placid pools and occasional rapids of
"Moon River".

HOMING

They come from distant oceans.
In ones and twos, in pods and shoals,
Silver as the sun's light, upon a sparkling sea,
They nose their way,
Back to freshwater;
Back to our rivers;
Back to the gravels,
Where they were born.

dj

Contents

Acknowledgments

No man is an island - and certainly not an angler or a writer. Along the way I have had support and encouragement from ghillies, scientists, writers, fellow-anglers and the organisations which work so hard to protect and manage Scotland's wild Atlantic salmon.

Dr Wendy Kenyon, NASCO; Professor Ken Whelan, The Atlantic Salmon Trust; Dr Alan Wells and Brian Davidson; Fisheries Management Scotland - have all been most helpful.

Many Fisheries Trusts and District Salmon Fishery Boards have shared their knowledge and fact-checked my interpretation of their work, specifically: Fay Hieatt and Dr Ronald Campbell, The Tweed Foundation; Dr Lorraine Hawkins and Edwin Third, River Dee Trust and Roger Knight, Spey Fisheries Board.

Welcome contributions have come from Luke Cumins and Rachel Coyle, Tweed Forum and from Dr Hamish Moir of Cbec Eco-engineering UK Ltd. Other quotations are acknowledged in the text and the References. Hydrograph data from the UK National River Flow Archive.

The Front Cover: "Salmon 'Loup'" and the other black-and-white drawings are by the late Colin Gibson. I have been permitted to share them through Colin's estate and the generous help of his daughter Gillian. Credits for other visuals are acknowledged in the text. Other photos and sketch maps by the author.

The Title Page: "Leaping Salmon" is reproduced by kind permission of The Estate of C.F. Tunnicliffe OBE, RA

My special thanks goes to Morny, my wife and fellow-traveller, for her patient proof-reading and editing and for putting up with life with an angler, a writer and a Pict. Any remaining errors and opinions are mine.

The International Year Of The Salmon

Environmental change and human impacts across the Northern Hemisphere are placing salmon at risk. The *International Year of the Salmon (IYS)* aims to bring people together to share and develop knowledge, raise awareness and take action on behalf of these fish.

The North Atlantic Salmon Conservation Organization (NASCO) is a key partner in IYS, taking part in a bold multi-year initiative in co-operation with the North Pacific Anadromous Fish Commission. Across the Northern Hemisphere an intense burst of outreach and research is underway. This aims to fill knowledge gaps and catalyse new ways to generate and share knowledge necessary for the resilience of salmon and people in a changing world. NASCO is an intergovernmental organisation. Its objectives are the conservation, restoration and rational management of wild Atlantic salmon stocks, which do not recognise national boundaries.

The extraordinary lifecycle of salmon exposes them to many environmental and human-caused risks in the North Atlantic, influencing their health and abundance. Despite the enormous efforts being made to conserve and restore wild Atlantic salmon, the International Council for the Exploration of the Sea (ICES) clearly indicates that abundance remains low – indeed, in some areas it is critically so.

IYS is an opportunity to catalyse the efforts being made to manage the species by raising awareness of what people can do to ensure salmon and their habitats are conserved and restored. A number of resources are available on the IYS website (www.yearofthesalmon.org)

Sarah Robinson, NASCO. 2018

"*To me there is nothing in all sport equal to the glory of success in salmon fishing, but the supreme moment is undoubtedly the actual hooking of the fish.*"

Grey of Fallodon. *"Fly Fishing"*

Introduction

Salmon numbers across the Northern Hemisphere, both in the Atlantic and the Pacific are now very low. In Scotland the angling catch in 2018 was the lowest since records began in 1952. What are the causes of this serious state of play and what is the future for Scotland's wild salmon? 2019 is the International Year of the Salmon - a coordinated response across both northern oceans to raise awareness of the plight of these iconic fish.

The causes of this situation are multiple and complex. Some problems are at sea. Some problems are around our coasts. Some are in the freshwater phase of the salmon's life cycle. Some of the problems are more controllable than others. Above all is the overarching challenge of climate change.

Years of research by fisheries biologists and others and hundreds of scientific papers have been produced trying to untangle the challenges of the salmon as a 'fish'. These are largely beyond the scope of this book and this author. Many of the challenges on the high seas are almost beyond our control. We have more control in the freshwater phase of the salmon's life cycle.

There is no doubt that salmon are not returning to Scottish rivers in the abundance of previous years. As an angler that concerns me. I am interested in why there are so few salmon - but also how changes in river conditions are affecting the fish and the enjoyment of my sport. As a geographer, I am interested in how the freshwater environment - the rivers, headwaters and the watersheds of the uplands - can help the salmon to thrive - especially in a future which is forecast to be dominated by a changing climate.

In September 2019 the Scottish Government published *Protecting Scotland's Future: the Government's Programme 2019-2020*. This included a commitment to establish a National Forum on Climate Change and to publish a multi-year national wild Atlantic salmon strategy by September 2020. It will have much to tackle!

CHAPTER 1

Salmon in a Changing Climate, 2007

"There is widespread agreement among fishery scientists that large, climatically-driven changes in the distribution and abundance of the crustaceans and young fish upon which salmon and sea trout feed are the primary reason for the current shortfall."

Dick Shelton, Atlantic Salmon Trust, 2007

Courtesy: Neil R Jamieson

In 2007 a number of seemingly unrelated events came to my attention:

- The members of the local angling association spent the first few weeks of the year clearing flood debris from their favourite fishing pools;

- The proprietor and ghillies of one of the lower beats of the River Tay delayed opening its salmon fishing for two weeks:
- Incoming reports of the Scottish grilse run in 2006 were of small and poorly-conditioned fish.
- A television news item reported salmon spawning redds washed away by winter floods.

Was there some common thread to these events? I started my research and this chapter is based upon an article published in *"Trout and Salmon"* magazine in July 2008.

"With the publication of the International Governmental Panel on Climate Change, Summary Report in February 2007 and the Stern Report in 2006, the scientific basis and the economic implications of climate change was coming into sharper focus. Even if some scientists could not agree on the cause and extent of climate change, there is a general consensus that the world is becoming a warmer place. Eleven of the twelve years between 1995 and 2006 were the warmest years on record.

- Winter 2006/07 was the warmest winter since records began;
- January 2007 was the warmest on record.

Even if mankind took steps to limit the future CO2 emissions the process already started would continue and get worse for several generations. While it might have been fanciful to dream of wading the Thames for tarpon or deep-sea fishing for marlin off Cornwall, there would be implications for our sport of salmon fishing. Some of these were already in evidence in the UK - with increasing water shortages, floods, gales and even tornadoes, regularly making the national headlines. These changes would affect the marine environment as well.

Already, by that time, the North Sea was measurably warmer, with effects on cold-water species such as cod. The North

Atlantic was more complicated with conflicting effects of warmer waters from the Gulf Stream opposing colder freshwater melting off the Greenland ice cap. These alterations would not only influence salmon in the sea, but also ultimately affect the broader ocean currents and the "conveyor belt" which drives the North Atlantic Drift itself. What did this mean for our salmon fisheries and our sport of angling. The prognosis was not very good.

The general view was that temperatures in United Kingdom could increase by 4 degrees C by 2080. In addition the forecasts were that:

- Summers would become hotter and drier, particularly in the south and east of Britain;
- Winters would become warmer and wetter, especially in the north and west;
- Rainfall would arrive in more intense events, such as summer thunderstorms or winter gales.
- There would be an increase in storminess, with increased wind speeds;

With hotter, drier summers there was likely to be increased pressure on both ground and surface water supplies. Agriculture, industry and domestic customers would all be looking for a share of the reduced water available. The warmer, drier conditions would also affect the insects on which young salmon feed. Some species, such as Yellow May, were already moving northwards and, as water and air temperatures increased, others species might follow. We might need to rethink our fly calendar to keep up with these changes.

The fish themselves might need to adapt to increasing temperatures. Salmon are essentially cold water fish and some of our shallow streams may get close to critical temperatures quite easily with adverse effects on juvenile survival. Drier summers would affect salmon runs and salmon fishing. Salmon migrations and "taking" behaviour are closely related to river flows. Low summer flows could delay salmon runs entering the river. Long periods of low river levels discourage salmon activity and occasional freshets are often needed for salmon to take the angler's fly. Low summer flows have been implicated in the late arrival of the grilse in many smaller rivers in 2006, although other factors might be at work here.

On the face of it, warmer, wetter winters might be welcomed. Higher water temperatures should allow insect life to continue activity and young salmon should continue to grow without the customary growth-check associated with low winter temperatures. But salmon are adapted to coping with low winter temperatures and have to adjust when it changes.

Already, Bob Laughton, biologist to the River Spey Trust, was finding a reduction in those young salmon which normally spend three years in the river before going to sea. The majority of parr already spent only two years in the river and an increasing number of smolts were going to sea after only one year in the river. The suggestion was that salmon parr, which previously took three years to grow to "smolting" size were growing to the required size in less time. This might seem a good idea but those smolts which used to stay three years growing in the river tended to live in the upper headwaters and are the ones which would normally return as 2- or 3-sea winter spring salmon - the very component of the salmon stock that is declining.

On the River Tay, for some years, there had been suspicions that the runs were getting later and that many more fresh-run salmon were entering the river after the end of the season on 15 October, than there were three decades ago. To find some evidence, David Summers, biologist to the Tay District Salmon Fisheries Board, carried out a fishing experiment during the close-season, up to 19 November 2005. The survey found that there were some fish, mainly grilse, still entering the Tay in late October/early November. However, these were only encountered in the lower reaches and, except for the lower

Earn, were a distinct minority. "While relatively few genuinely fresh fish were caught in the survey this is not to say late-run fish are not an insignificant part of the Tay salmon population", David reported, and continued "In the first two days of the 2006 season on one lower Tay beat, 15 fish were caught which had still to spawn, half of which were described as "bright silver", one of which was sea-liced". In 2007 one lower beat delayed opening by two weeks to avoid catching un-spawned fish.

More intense rainfall events mean more floods, possibly dirty, flashy, short-duration spates, which might bring high, coloured water through your fishing beat at short notice. During hotter, drier summers these spates could be a blessing but like "snow on a railway line" it was likely to be the "wrong kind" of spate.

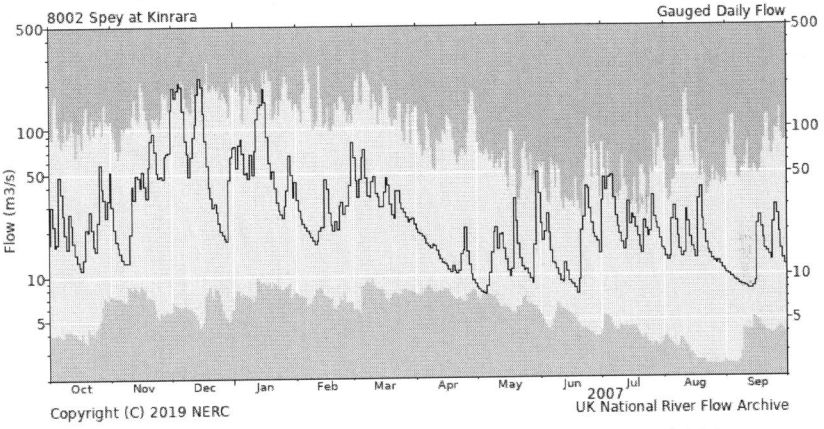

Spey catchment - series of high flows, winter 2006/2007
Data from the UK National River Flow Archive

Note: The daily mean flows (measured in m3s-1) together with the maximum and minimum daily flows prior to September 2007 (shown by the shaded areas). Daily flows falling outside the maximum/minimum range are indicated where the bold trace enters the shaded areas.

Some of these spates in winter were already intense enough to shift significant amounts of gravel. "In some spawning tributaries," said Bob Laughton, "most of the gravels have been shifted down into the main stem. The spawning is OK there but there is a waste of spawning space in the smaller tributary." Winter floods have other damaging qualities. Winter floods on the Conon washed salmon eggs out of redds which had already been completed. This represented a great loss of the following year's fry and parr and to returning adult salmon in 2 to 5 year's time. The cost to the fishery can be imagined.

A short, sharp spate on the Feugh

Traditionally, the spring fishing on the Spey benefited from the snow melting from the corries and plateaux of the Cairngorm Mountains. These tended to maintain good, steady river levels through April, May and even into June. With less winter snow accumulating on the Cairngorms, the steady snow melt was being replaced by more flashy spates from irregular rainfall in the mountains.

A Warming Sea

If sea temperatures were increasing, what would this mean for salmon? Salmon use the sea for feeding and growth. Changes in sea temperature which affect their food supply would affect their size, condition and timing when they enter our rivers. Over previous years the major concern in salmon conservation circles had been the poor marine survival in the

North Atlantic. Despite all the improvements to the salmon's freshwater environment, the export of good quantities of smolts to sea and the reduction in interceptory netting, the percentage of adult salmon returning to our rivers had been so poor that the phrase "Lost at Sea" has almost been an epitaph.

In his article in the Atlantic Salmon Trust *Winter Review 2006/2007,* Dick Shelton, Research Director of Atlantic Salmon Trust, reached a conclusion as to the role of climate change:

> "There is widespread agreement among fishery scientists", he said, "that large, climatically-driven changes in the distribution and abundance of the crustaceans and young fish upon which salmon and sea trout feed are the primary reason for the current shortfall." "Shortages of spring-running salmon," he continued, "appear to reflect major reductions in the availability of suitable food organisms in the waters of the north west Atlantic. Almost certainly, similar factors underlie both the small average size and the later run timing of the current year's summer grilse run, but in this instance the problem is likely to lie nearer home in the waters of the Norwegian Sea."

Chris Todd, Professor of Marine Ecology at St Andrews University was more specific. He had studied the "small grilse" phenomenon since 1993 and concluded that a temperature anomaly in the Norwegian Sea – more specifically based on a central point at 67.5 degrees N; 4.5 degrees W – was to blame. He believed that a mid-winter warming of the ocean where the grilse feed, correlated with the decreasing size and poor condition of returning grilse. This had implications for the way we conserved our grilse. Todd was concerned that:

> "Some grilse sampled in 2006 were more than 30% underweight and many of these small, thin grilse may not survive in freshwater to spawn. Those that do are carrying fewer eggs than their predecessors." "Many more of these

smaller fish need to spawn in order to maintain egg numbers," he continues, " consequently we need to wean anglers off the notion that grilse are relatively unimportant and ensure that as many of these fish as possible are released back into the water. ...... grilse are an important component of our fisheries and they need protection from over-exploitation".

These, then, were some of the possible impacts of climate change on our sport - observed or forecast in 2007. Increasing rainfall intensity, frequency of storms and droughts would all affect the stability of our salmon rivers and the opportunities for serious angling. There may have been other threats. Some of them might not have happened - but some did!

First published in *Trout and Salmon* - July 2008

Update for 2019

In 2018, the Meteorological Office, reported the seventh warmest year for the United Kingdom since 1884. The 21st century so far had, overall, been warmer than the previous three centuries. For the most recent decade (2009-2018) United Kingdom summers had been on average 13% wetter than 1961-1990 and United Kingdom winters had been 12% wetter than the same period. By 2050, there would be a 50% chance of having summers as warm as that of 2018.

In 2019 there is broad consensus that climate change is a likely driver of major significance for salmon, with effects being felt at very broad scales and in different ways. There are trends for general ocean warming, but there is also potential for short-term or single-year anomalous 'big' events having high impact. Climate change impacts on salmon populations are likely to be spread over several parts of the life cycle, with responses to changes in river growth, growth at sea and hence overall year-class survival..

CHAPTER 2

Born To Survive
The Life Cycle of the Atlantic Salmon

"But at recurring intervals, say three to five minutes, each female would suddenly fling herself flat on her silvery broadside, usually athwart the stream, and thereupon followed a sort of convulsive spasm, her whole frame writhing as if in agony, while her tail, lashing out in vertical strokes, sent the water flying in spray."

Abel Chapman, "The Borders and Beyond"

Similar scenes may be found in the headwaters of many rivers from October to January as the Atlantic salmon gather on the spawning grounds.

A suitable spawning area has certain physical requirements. The gravel must be of a size which allows it to be moved by the salmon and must provide a free flow of water through the incubating spawn. It must be free of fine sediment which would clog up the interstices between the stones and reduce the flow. The water itself must be clean and must flow at a speed which is sufficient to provide adequate circulation yet not so fast as to wash away the gravel or spawn. These physical conditions restrict the areas which are suitable for salmon spawning and in any river system there are usually well-defined spawning gravels which are favoured by the fish.

The eggs are laid in a hollow in the gravel, called a 'redd', which is scooped out by the female fish. Each hen fish will produce between 500 and 800 eggs for each pound of her body weight so that a 10 lb salmon should lay something in the order of 5000 to 8000 eggs. As the eggs are being laid by the female they are fertilised by the 'milt' shed by the male lying alongside. After spawning the eggs are covered with gravel and the spent adult fish are known as 'kelts'.

Although death is not the inevitable result of spawning, as it is in the case of the Pacific salmon, many kelts, particularly the males, do not survive to make the downstream journey to the sea. Observations on the Conon river system suggest that something between 20% and 36% of the upstream run eventually returns downstream as kelts. Once they have reached the sea the kelts are still liable to be eaten by seals, but they have at least the opportunity to regain their condition and to make another spawning run at a future date. Those fish which are spawning for a second time form a variable proportion of the upstream run but figures of between 3% and 6% have been recorded.

The eggs hatch in the Spring to form the next stage of the life cycle, the "alevin", with a yolk sac attached to its underside. The alevin remains in the gravel until its yolk sac is used up when it emerges as a "fry" into the nursery stream some four weeks later. This is a period of very high mortality due to predation, starvation and competition for space and it is estimated that less than 10% of the eggs survive to become viable fry. The fry stage lasts for about a year during which time the fish grow until they can be called "parr". The parr remains feeding and growing in freshwater until it is two or three years old and has attained a size of between 10 and 15 cm.

Salmon spawning grounds on a tributary of the Dee
Courtesy: River Dee Trust

Off to Sea

In the early summer of the second or third year the parr assumes a silvery coat and migrates downstream to the sea as a "smolt". This smolt migration generally takes place during May and June and is again a time of high mortality. Fish-eating birds such as the goosander, merganser and cormorant take their toll while predator fish, from pike to cod, also feed on the smolts in the river and in the sea. Once in the sea the smolt population appears to divide into two sections. One section remains in closer waters while the other section starts out on the deep sea migrations for which the salmon is famous. Both sections however feed voraciously on plankton, crustaceans and sand-eels and grow from smolts of a few ounces to about 5 lb during the first year at sea.

The section of the smolt population which returns to the river the following summer is known as "grilse". The average weight of the grilse is around 5 lb but it is sexually mature and contributes to the spawning stock one year after leaving the river. The other section of the smolt population will remain in the sea for more than one winter, almost doubling in weight each year, and will return to freshwater as "salmon" proper. Tagging experiments have been carried out on Scottish rivers for many years and indicate that one of the main feeding grounds during this marine phase lies off the south-east coast of Greenland.

The salmon 'proper' will return to freshwater at weights of up to 80 lb and there is even a legendary report of a fish of more than 100 lb being caught in the Forth. Both salmon and grilse exhibit a distinct homing tendency and usually return to the river from which they departed as smolts. There are records of fish which have been found in rivers other than their parent stream but it is a general rule that they return to the river of their origin.

Homing

When the homing fish return on their spawning run they become the quarry of the angler. They enter the rivers fresh from the sea, silver in colour, with sea-lice on their flanks and full of the strength of their sea feeding. These "fresh-run" fish represent the cream of the angling. As they approach the rivers the salmon cease to feed and rely on their store of energy to sustain their upstream journey. This poses the controversial question as to why a salmon takes an angler's lure. There are probably as many theories for this as there are anglers but, suffice to say, while all the evidence points to the fact that salmon do not feed in freshwater, they can be induced to eat or attack a worm, an artificial fly or an imitation fish.

After some time in fresh water, salmon gradually lose their silvery colour and the rigours of the upstream journey sap their condition. Towards the end of the summer the males grow red in colour and develop hooked under-jaws called "kypes". The females grow dark and almost black as spawning approaches and the flesh grows soft, pale and barely edible. By the time spawning takes place, the fish are a shadow of their former selves. They are scarred, discoloured, often diseased, with their fins ragged and torn. The final act of spawning is often fatal and those that survive may not make it all the way downstream to the sea.

But, if all goes well, each spring a new generation of salmon will emerge from the gravel and start the process all over again.

First published in *The Haig Guide to Salmon Fishing in Scotland,* 1981

Update for 2019

As described later, changes to the freshwater and marine phases of the salmon's life-cycle have evolved, probably connected to climate change.

CHAPTER 3

Where the Wild Salmon Run
Scotland's Salmon Rivers

"A river is water in its loveliest form. Rivers have life and sound and movement and infinity of variation. Rivers are veins of the earth through which the life blood returns to the heart."

Roderick Haig-Brown, *"A River Never Sleeps"*

Second in importance only to the salmon itself, is the river in which we pursue it. As anglers, we enjoy the river for a far longer time than we enjoy the salmon. We savour its moods and colours from the moment we arrive at the waterside until we leave it, and often, in the mind's eye, for much longer. We may perhaps enjoy the salmon only for those few intoxicating minutes of capture - if we are successful. The river itself is a vital part of the fishing experience and to know about the river is as interesting as to know about the salmon. Roderick Haig-Brown, in his classic book *"A River Never Sleeps"*, encapsulates the magical properties of a salmon river. How often have we surveyed the river and wondered why it chose this course rather than that one? Why does this part thunder through a narrow gorge and that part sweep across a wide strath? Why does this stream rise and fall with the rain and the other runs steady even in drought? The answers to these questions lead us away from the salmon itself and into the realms of the rocks, the rain and the geological past.

The Physical Regions

A glance at the map shows Scotland to be made up of three major physical regions each characterised by different rocks, scenery and rivers. The Highlands, the Central Lowlands and the Southern Uplands are each separated from the other by great geological cracks   - the Highland Boundary Fault and the Southern Uplands Fault.

The Highlands are composed of very old, hard rocks of Cambrian and pre-Cambrian age - metamorphic gneisses, schists, quartzites and granites. Over the aeons of geological time these rocks have been folded and faulted along a distinct trend from south-west to north-east to form the ancient Caledonian mountain chain. Subsequent erosion and uplift leaves its present shape as a series of high plateaux and ridges exceeding 4000 ft in Ben Nevis and the Cairngorms, deeply dissected by such rivers as the Conon, Beauly, Spey, Dee and Tay.

The Southern Uplands are formed of slightly younger rocks of Ordovician and Silurian age. The characteristic shales, mudstones and 'greywackes' have also been extensively folded and faulted by later earth movements and once again they follow the south-west to north-east Caledonian trend. Uplift and erosion here has preserved remnant plateaux around 2600 ft in Cheviot, Broad Law and Merrick into which have been incised the valleys of the Tweed and Solway.

The Central Lowlands represent a great rift valley which has dropped down between the two great faults to north and south and has preserved much younger, softer rocks like the characteristic Old Red Sandstone of the Devonian period and the important Coal Measures and limestones of the Carboniferous. Many of the Highland rivers finish their course in the Central Lowlands, among them, the Tay, Earn, Forth and the North and South Esks of Angus.

The Highlands - The Upper Dee in the Cairngorms
Courtesy: River Dee Trust

Apart from the Central Lowlands there are other smaller lowland areas carved out of the younger rocks around the periphery of the mountain areas. The plain of Caithness, drained by the Thurso and the inner Moray Firth drained by the lower reaches of the Conon, Beauly, Ness, Nairn, Findhorn and Spey. Both lowlands mark the outcrops of Old Red Sandstone in the north. In the south, these younger rocks are picked out by the Merse of the Tweed and the valleys of the Annan and Nith.

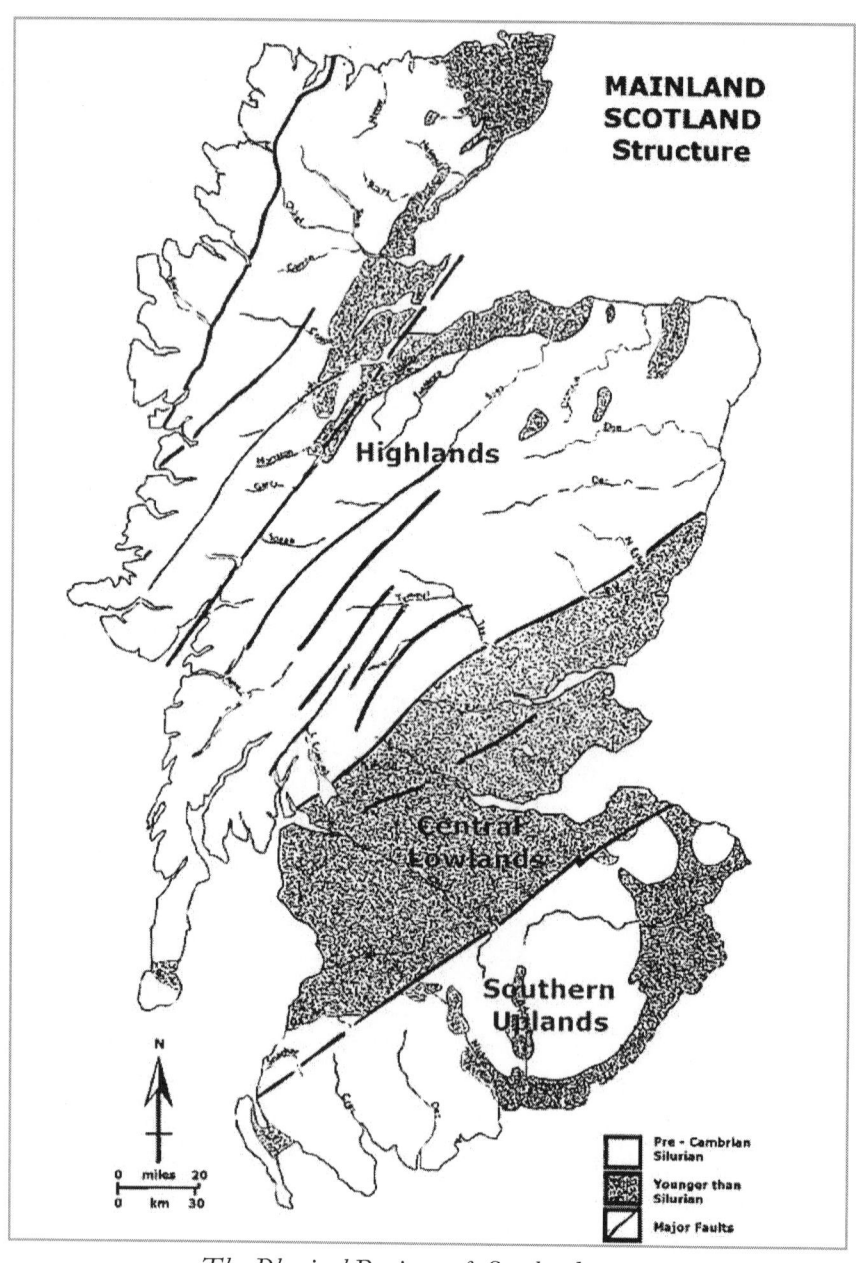

The Physical Regions of Scotland

How the Rivers Were Formed

Upon this varied structure and shape, flow the great salmon rivers, all of them owing something of their character and variety to the rocks beneath. How can we interpret the present drainage pattern? Rivers of all sizes apparently flow in many different directions with the only common denominator being their destination - the sea. However, a pattern can be identified. Two basic threads form the weft and the woof of the tapestry of Scotland's rivers The fundamental "Caledonian" grain of the rocks is reflected in a south-west to north-east orientation of many rivers and lochs. Working along lines of geological weakness such Highland waters as the Beauly, Ness, Nairn, Findhorn, Spey, Loch Awe and Loch Tay are paralleled by the Lowland rivers of Isla, Allan, Devon and Tyne and the Southern Upland rivers of Girvan, Stinchar, Ettrick, Yarrow and Teviot.

However, superimposed upon this structurally-related pattern is a contrasting and much older pattern of rivers which flow across the grain of the land "discordant" to the underlying structure. This is a predominantly eastwards or south-eastwards flowing drainage system which is exemplified by such rivers as the Shin, Conon, Garry and Moriston, the Don and the Dee, the North and South Esks, the Tummel/Tay, the Forth and the upper Tweed.

While there is still much discussion about the exact pattern and mechanism for the formation of this original 'discordant' drainage, the widely accepted theory visualises some eastward-sloping land surface that was formed, either by an uplifted dome of chalk strata or by some uplifted erosion platform carved into the older rocks by the seas of earlier times. Upon this generally eastward-sloping surface, the primeval rains fell and coalesced into the early rivers, running from an original watershed not too far removed from the present one and out into what is now the North Sea. By subsequent uplift and long erosion any younger rocks have now been stripped off most of the land and the old river pattern is now incised down into the underlying rocks as a pattern of discordant rivers.

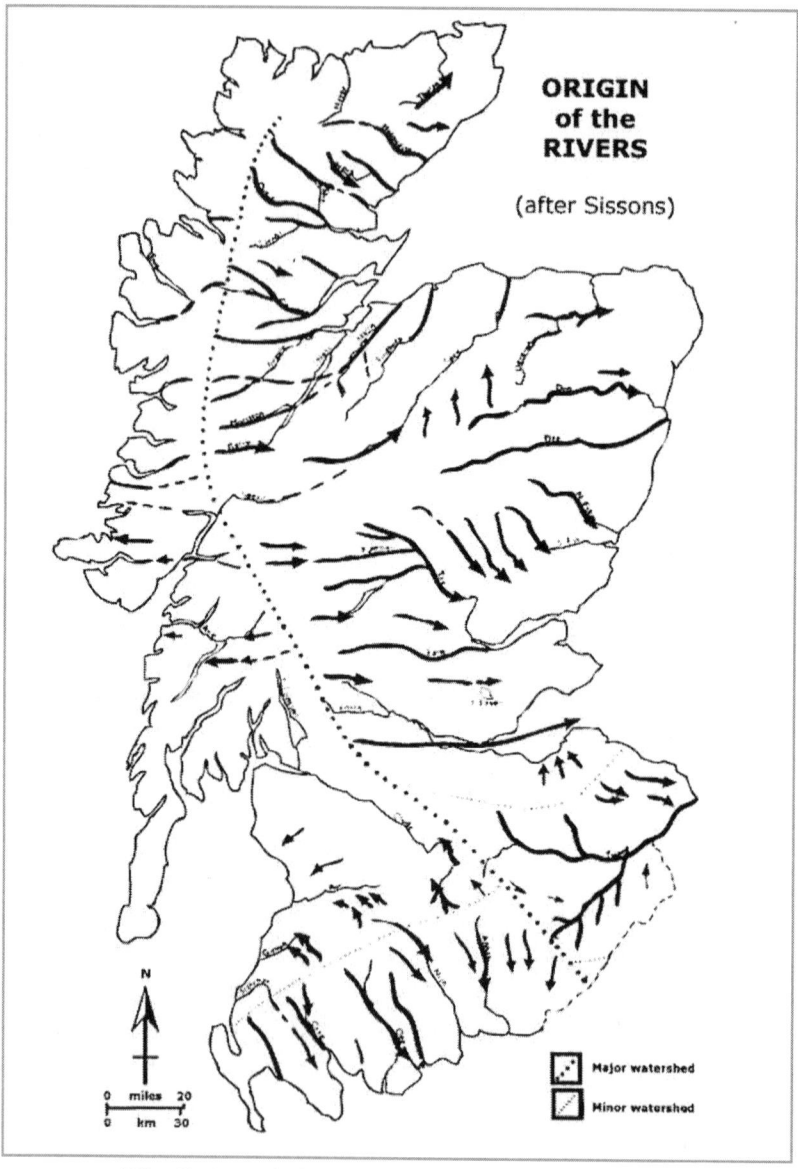

The Origin of Scotland's Rivers. (After Sissons)

The Effects of the Ice Age

The detailed features of our rivers, which catch the eye and excite the imagination of the curious angler today, appeared in the last few seconds of geological time - from the last Ice Age or, more correctly, from the last glaciation of the Pleistocene Era. During this time a vast ice sheet spread out from a main centre in the Highlands to cover the whole of Scotland, at one stage, and then with later contractions and re-advances the ice affected progressively less of the country. This ice movement and the associated meltwaters are responsible for most of the detailed features which dominate the valleys through which the salmon rivers flow. The high corries of the upper Spey, the loch-filled rock basins of the Ness, Tay and Awe and the steep-sided, flat bottomed valleys of the Conon and Beauly are all evidence of the erosive gouging and plucking of the ice.

All this material had to be transported and deposited somewhere else and once again most of the river valleys show evidence of this aspect of glaciation. The retreating glaciers dumped large piles of angular fragments in the form of "moraines" which often stretched right across the valleys and sometimes formed dams for melt-water lakes. Other debris has been moved and sorted by melt-water streams to form long linear ridges of gravel called "eskers" or mounds known as "kames". Many lower valleys are littered with these features. Variations in post-glacial sea level have left river terraces representing former flood-plains perched high above the present river levels. These are particularly evident on the Findhorn, Spey and Tay while ice-dammed lakes have left ancient shorelines in Glen Spean and in the 'Parallel Roads' of Glen Roy.

Just Add Water

Within these channels of eroded bedrock or deposited gravel runs the water itself, always different in colour, clarity, height and speed. Each day, each hour brings some subtle change in the water or in the reflected sky from where it comes. This restless sky is the result of Scotland's position in the battleground between the warm air of the Tropics and the cold polar air from the Arctic; between the moist air of the Atlantic Ocean and the dry winds of continental Europe. Four characteristic air masses affect the Scottish weather. The cool moist polar maritime air mass moves from its source in the North Atlantic on north-westerly winds and, becoming unstable over the Gulf Stream, sets off big showery cumulus and cumulo-nimbus clouds in an otherwise clear sky. From the other direction comes the warm, moist tropical maritime air from the region of the Azores. Cooling and stabilising as it moves from the south-west this usually gives rise to mild, muggy conditions of low stratus clouds, hill fog and drizzle - the apocryphal 'scotch mist' and 'smirr' of rain.

Where these two maritime air masses meet along the Polar Front, a series of warm-sector depressions develop and Scotland's changeable weather can often be analysed as a progression of wet, warm fronts and mild, drier warm-sectors, followed by showery cold fronts in seemingly endless procession from the west. Settled weather is not unknown in Scotland when the dry continental air from Europe drifts over as an anticyclone, bringing cold snaps in winter and heat-waves in summer.

The sum total of all this frantic weather activity can be measured, as far as the angler is concerned, in terms of rainfall on the land and runoff to the rivers. Rainfall, or more correctly, precipitation - which includes snowfall - is extremely variable across Scotland. In the western mountains a peak of 5000 mm contrasts with a low of 600 mm on the east coast. Most of the precipitation on the west coast is in the form of rain from the moist south-westerly winds, lifting and condensing on the high mountain walls with rapid runoff into the characteristic spate rivers of the west coast. In the central and eastern parts of the Grampians by contrast much of the precipitation falls as snow which lies in many areas for more than 100 days in the year and may lie on the high tops of the Cairngorms all the year round. This snowmelt traditionally keeps water flowing in the Spey and the Dee well into the summer. Climate change is already having an impact on this traditional pattern of weather.

But these are our rivers - their sources, their nature and their problems. They form a resource which is as valuable and interesting as it is beautiful - fitting habitats for the salmon.

First published in *The Haig Guide to Salmon Fishing in Scotland,* 1981

Update for 2019

As described later, changes in weather patterns of temperatures and rainfall are apparently changing the flow regimes of many rivers - although the rocks and the rivers remain!

CHAPTER 4

A Protected Species
The C.A.S.S. Project, 2004-2008

"….to safeguard and maintain the abundance and diversity of salmon in Scotland through the significant improvement of freshwater habitats, the development of management guidelines and the promotion and demonstration of best practice in removal of key threats through joint working and partnership."

Scottish Natural Heritage/LIFE-Fund

Scottish Natural Heritage is responsible for the conservation of species and habitats in Scotland. One of its duties is implementing the European Union Habitats Directive which protect species and habitats which are deemed to be of conservation concern across the European Union. The Atlantic salmon, *Salmo salar,* while in freshwater and several important salmon rivers are protected in Scotland because of this legislation. Adopted in 1992, the "EU Habitats Directive" ensures the conservation of a wide range of rare, threatened or endemic animal and plant species. The Directive is now part of United Kingdom law and The Habitats Regulations implement the Habitats Directive in Scotland. They provide protection to European protected species and Natura sites i.e. Special Protection Areas for Wild Birds (SPA) and Special Areas of Conservation (SAC). As part of this process, the Atlantic salmon while in freshwater is listed, together with other fish: river lamprey, allis shad, twaite shad, vendace and powan

Fifteen of Scotland's rivers have been designated as Special Areas of Conservation. These are the Bladnoch, Borgie, Dee, Evelix, Kerry, Moidart, Moriston, Naver, Oykel, South Esk, Spey, Tay, Teith, Thurso and Tweed. In 2004, seven of these rivers - Oykel, Moriston, Spey, South Esk, Tay, Tweed and Bladnoch – which collectively constitute approximately 38% of Scotland's Atlantic salmon resource were identified to be part of the Conservation of Atlantic Salmon in Scotland (CASS) project.

This project finished in July 2008, marking the end of one of the biggest Atlantic salmon conservation projects in Scotland if not in Europe. The CASS project was financed by the European Union LIFE-Nature fund and managed by Scottish Natural Heritage. It involved seventeen partner organisations and nine co-financiers in addition to the European Commission. The overall objective of the project was:

"to safeguard and maintain the abundance and diversity of salmon in Scotland through the significant improvement of freshwater habitats, the development of management guidelines and the promotion and demonstration of best practice in removal of key threats through joint working and partnership."

Interpreting the Euro-speak, this means a better life-style for salmon in Scottish rivers and good lessons to be shared around.

Reasons for Designation

These eight rivers are not designated as Special Areas of Conservation solely for the importance of their salmon. Only the Bladnoch is designated solely for its Atlantic salmon, Salmo salar. The Oykel and the Moriston are designated primarily for their freshwater pearl mussel, *Margaritifera margaritifera* with salmon as a secondary qualification. The mussel and the salmon populations are of equal importance in the South Esk. The Spey, Dee and Tay share the interest between the mussel, the salmon and the European otter, *Lutra lutra,* while the Spey, Tweed and Tay are also important for sea lamprey, *Petromyzon marinus.* and the Tay and Tweed for the brook lamprey, *Lampetra planeri,* and the river lamprey, *Lampetra fluvialis.*

The close relationship between Atlantic salmon and the freshwater pearl mussel in these rivers may seem strange until the ecology of the pearl mussel is understood. The life cycle of the freshwater pearl mussel is complex, involving a compulsory stage as a parasite, called a *glochidium,* on the gills of either a salmon or trout juvenile. Except for their parasitic phase, mussels live buried, or partly buried, in sand and gravel in fast-flowing, unpolluted rivers and streams. They reach maturity at about 12 to 15 years of age and if left undisturbed they can live for more than 100 years. So the mussel is dependent on the salmon or another salmonid. In return the mussel is capable of filtering pollutants out of the water thus helping to purify the water on which salmon also depend. Both require clean water, free from silt. So what helps one, helps the other! At the beginning of the project the main threats to Atlantic salmon in Scottish rivers were perceived as:

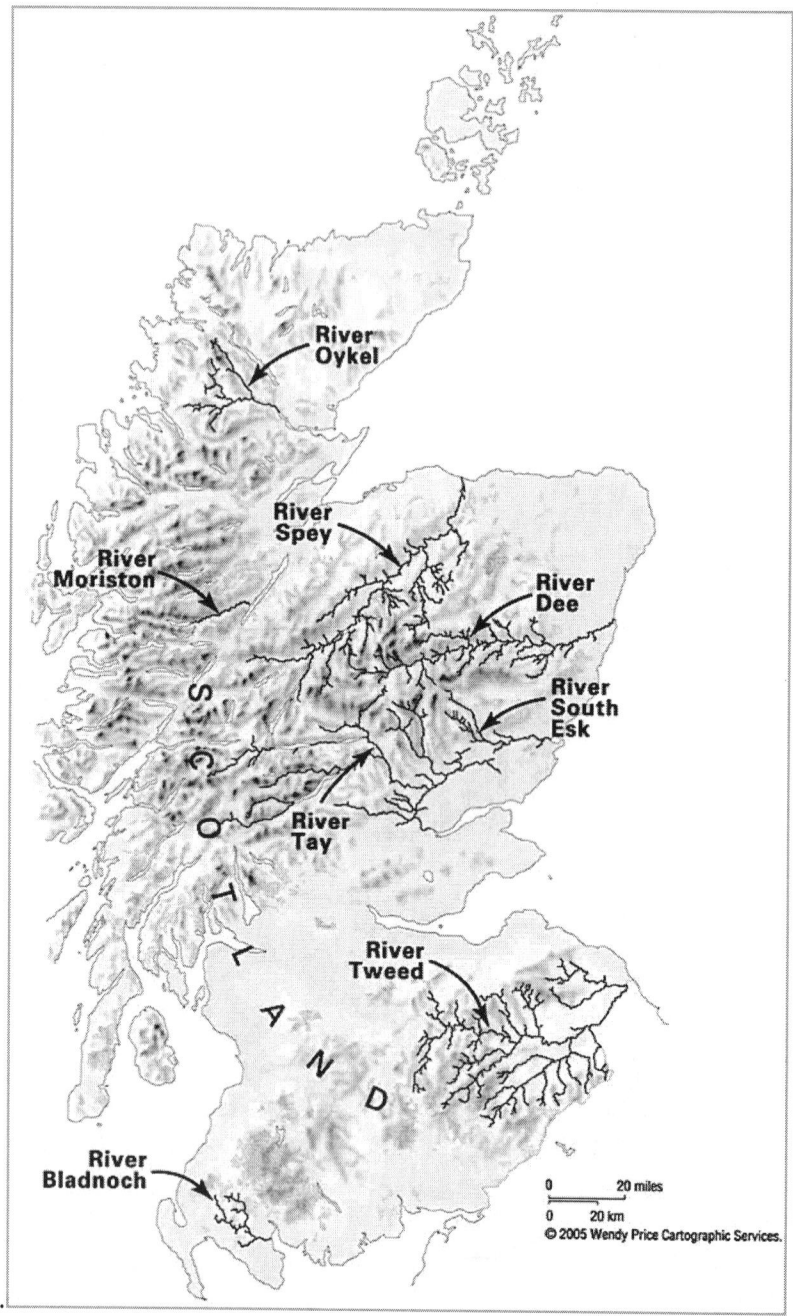

The C.A.S.S. Rivers

Courtesy: Scottish Natural Heritage

- The exploitation of salmon stocks by netting operations;
- The obstruction of river access by man-made obstacles;
- The degradation of in-stream and riparian habitat and siltation of river beds;
- The slow natural re-colonisation of newly accessible or restored stretches of river;
- The poor recognition of the value of positive conservation management and of the European Union Natura programmes by river stakeholders

The C.A.S.S. Rivers

The South Esk at Cortachy

The *Oykel* is a long, meandering river in the northern Highlands flowing into the Kyle of Sutherland on the east coast. The river supports an excellent, high-quality freshwater pearl mussel population with high densities recorded at some locations, including a bed numbering several thousand individuals. The Atlantic salmon is only a qualifying feature, but not a primary reason for site selection. The CASS activities identified for the Oykel and managed by the Kyle of Sutherland District Salmon Fishery Board and Scottish and Southern

Energy included electro-fishing surveys of juvenile salmon, the provision of a fish counter and screens at Duchally power station and purchasing the fishing rights of the estuary netting station to manage all salmon harvesting by rod and line.

The *Moriston* is another salmon river which is designated primarily because of its freshwater mussel population. Salmon-related work carried out by the Ness District Salmon Fishery Board and Scottish and Southern Energy include surveys of juvenile salmon and mussels.

The *Spey* is a large east coast river that drains an extensive upland catchment. It has several qualifications for SAC designation, including freshwater pearl mussel population, European otter and the sea lamprey in addition to the Atlantic salmon. The Spey supports one of the largest Atlantic salmon populations in Scotland with little evidence of modification by non-native stocks. Adults spawn throughout virtually the whole length of the river, and good quality nursery habitat is found in abundance in the main river and numerous tributaries. Salmon in the Spey system are little affected by artificial barriers to migration, and the waters in the catchment are largely unpolluted (the river is oligotrophic throughout its length)

The salmon population includes fish of all ages including migrating smolts and returning adults, possibly reflecting genetic differences within the Spey stock. Activities under the CASS project have been carried out by the Spey District Salmon Fishery Board, Scottish and Southern Energy, Moray Council, Transport Scotland and Forestry Commission Scotland. Key actions included installing fish counters and fish passes at Spey Dam and Mortlach, installing a fish counter and screens at Truim together with a smolt curtain at Tromie. Six obstructions caused by culverts and bridge aprons were removed to allow access to new spawning and nursery grounds.

The River Spey at Boat of Garden

The *Dee* is a major east coast river, which flows uninterrupted for some 130 km from its upland reaches in the high Cairngorms to the North Sea. In addition to its importance for freshwater mussels and otters, the River Dee supports a high-quality Atlantic salmon population in a river draining a large catchment on the east coast of Scotland. There is a weak nutrient gradient along its length, but it is essentially a nutrient-poor river. The high proportion of the river accessible to salmon has resulted in it supporting the full range of life-history types found in Scotland, with sub-populations of spring, summer salmon and grilse all being present. The headwaters which drain the southern Cairngorm and northern Grampian mountains are particularly important for multi sea-winter spring salmon, but there has been a significant decline in their abundance in recent years.

The extensive areas accessible to salmon means the River Dee supports a significant proportion of the Scottish salmon resource. In recent years it has contributed about 4% or 5% of all salmon caught in Scotland. Activities under CASS were carried out by the Dee District Salmon Fishery Board and Forestry Commission Scotland. These included catchment and riparian habitat surveys, the fencing of stream-side habitat to reduce siltation, the installation of silt traps and the coppicing and planting of broadleaved trees. Obstructions were overcome and 3 fish passes were installed on tributaries to open up new salmon habitat.

River Dee - A spring salmon is returned

Courtesy: River Dee Trust

In addition to abundant freshwater mussels the *South Esk* supports a large, high-quality salmon population in a river draining a moderate-sized catchment on the east coast of Scotland. It has a strong nutrient gradient along its length, rising in the nutrient-poor Grampians and flowing for half of its length through the rich agricultural lands of Strathmore. The high proportion of the South Esk which is accessible to salmon and the range of ecological conditions in the river allows it to support the full range of life-history types found in Scotland, with sub-populations of spring, summer salmon and grilse all being present. CASS activities were undertaken by the Esks

District Salmon Fishery Board and included juvenile and habitat surveys and extensive fencing of riparian habitat in the upper catchment to control grazing and reduce siltation.

The *Tay* supports a high-quality Atlantic salmon population, with rod catch returns showing that the Tay is consistently one of the top three salmon rivers in Scotland. In 1999 the catch was 7230 fish, over 10% of the Scottish total.

Harling on the River Tay

The Tay drains a very large catchment, and has the greatest flow of all United Kingdom rivers. There is considerable ecological variety in the Tay catchment, resulting in the Tay supporting the full range of salmon life-history types found in Scotland with adult salmon entering the River Tay throughout the year to spawn in different parts of the catchment. Other species qualifying for Special Area of Conservation status include the otter, the sea lamprey, brook lamprey and the river lamprey. CASS actions have focussed on the Tay District Salmon Fishery Board, Scottish and Southern Energy and Scottish Natural Heritage and have included modifications to the fish passes at Lochay and Gaur to improve access for salmon and the addition of a counter at Stronuich. A major output has been the creation of a *Code of Practice for Gravel Extraction* on the Tay to protect spawning areas, with a view to creating a Scotland-wide Best Practice guide on gravel extraction and dredging on salmon rivers.

Tweed is the best example in Britain of a large river showing a strong nutrient gradient along its length, with nutrient-poor conditions in its headwaters and nutrient-rich lowland conditions just before it enters the sea at Berwick. In addition to its otters, sea lampreys, brook lampreys and river lampreys Tweed supports a very large, high-quality salmon population in a river which drains a large catchment on the east coast with sub-catchments in both Scotland and England. The high proportion of the River Tweed accessible to salmon, and the variety of habitat conditions in the river, has resulted in the Scottish section of the river supporting the full range of salmon life-history types, with sub-populations of spring, summer salmon and grilse all being present.

The extensive system supports a significant proportion of the Scottish salmon resource. In recent years, the salmon catch in the River Tweed has been the highest in Scotland, with up to 15% of all salmon caught. Considerable work has been done by the Scottish Environment Protection Agency and the Tweed Foundation in tackling pollution and easing the passage of salmon through artificial barriers in the river. This has reversed many of the river's historical problems with water quality and access for salmon. CASS actions were carried out by the Tweed Foundation and focussed on the establishment of a VAKI fish counter on the Gala Water to monitor salmon stocks on this Tweed tributary.

The *Bladnoch* supports a high-quality salmon population in south-west Scotland, which unusually for rivers in this area, still supports a spring run of salmon. The river drains a moderate-sized catchment with both upland and lowland areas, and this variety is reflected in the river's ecological and water quality characteristics. Problems in the river's headwaters arise from acidification but national and local initiatives are both reducing and ameliorating the worst effects of this pollution source. CASS actions have been implemented by the Galloway Fisheries Trust, the Bladnoch District Salmon Fishery Board and Forestry Commission Scotland. They have focussed on forest re-structuring to reduce the effects of acidification together with riparian habitat management and bank protection to reduce siltation. Other work has involved electro-fishing, smolt-trapping and developing the hatchery for restocking and kelt-reconditioning. A major achievement has been acquiring a 99-year lease of the estuary netting rights to manage all salmon harvesting by rod and line.

Summary of Achievements

So what has CASS achieved for its 4.576 m euro investment. Over the four-year period the LIFE project has managed to:

- Halt the remaining commercial netting of salmon on the Oykel and the Bladnoch;
- Remove or bypass 25 obstacles improving access for salmon to 150 km of habitat on the Oykel, Spey, Moriston and Tay;
- Improve over 70,137 km of freshwater habitat for spawning and juvenile salmon;
- Control grazing along 80.6 km of river to improve river habitat and protect river banks;
- Stabilise 500 m of eroding riverbank and reduce siltation from surface runoff into two rivers South Esk and Bladnoch;
- Extend and diversify riparian woodland habitat along Spey, Dee and Bladnoch rivers;
- Re-stock restored areas of habitat with local populations of wild salmon on Spey and Bladnoch;
- Provide general guidance and a local Code of Practice for gravel extraction in salmon rivers, based on the River Tay.

Awareness and Education

One of the key tasks of the project was to raise awareness of salmon conservation and EU Natura issues with river owners and the public. This has been carried out, in one form or another, on all eight river projects. *Salmon in the Classroom* has been a key tool in this part of the project. The CASS project developed a *Salmon in the Classroom* website in March 2006 and initiated training for practitioners. Six rivers - Oykel, Moriston, Spey, Esk, Tay and Bladnoch – have majored on *Salmon in the Classroom* programmes, involving a total of 20 primary schools. Future generations of children should better appreciate the needs of salmon and safeguard the future of salmon angling.

First published in *The Salmon of Wisdom* (CD) 2009

CHAPTER 5

Salmon Come To Parliament
A Cause for Concern?

Autumn on Bemersyde, Tweed

In 2018 the rod-catches of salmon in Scotland were the lowest since records began in 1952. The total reported rod catch of wild salmon and grilse was 37,196, representing only 67% - two-thirds - of the previous 5-year average. Scottish anglers were not surprised, having suffered fruitless days of fishing throughout the season, but the figures were a shock to many others, including Scotland's parliamentarians.

On 4 April 2019, Rachael Hamilton, a Member of the Scottish Parliament, from Tweed-side, introduced a debate in the Scottish Parliament on the *"Long-term Decline in Salmon Stocks"*. Parliament was asked to note:

"...the reported long-term decline in salmon stocks across Scotland's major rivers, including the Tweed, the Spey, the Dee and the Tay; understands that catches have decreased over the last decade; notes that, on the Tweed, rod catches have fallen from 23,219 in 2012 to 6,577 in 2017; believes that this is marginally above the previous worst years, 1977 and 1980; understands that angling in Scotland supports around 2,800 jobs and contributes £100 million to the economy; acknowledges that fishing generates significant employment opportunities in rural areas; recognises that there are significant challenges ahead if salmon stocks are to return to previous levels, and notes the calls for the Scottish Government to take urgent action to devise effective conservation and management plans in conjunction with relevant bodies to help address what it sees as the persistent decline in salmon stocks."

The situation was sufficiently serious for one of Tweed's most experienced ghillies, Ian Farr, working on the Bemersyde beat for 32 years, to make a representation to the debate. In summary, Ian made the case that:

• Fish population decline on Scotland's salmon rivers is so significant this could be the last generation of salmon fishing as we know it;
• Tourism and the local economy are already being affected;
• Predation is an important factor in the decline;
• Immediate action can be taken to mitigate the situation.

In more detail, Ian submitted:

"Fish Numbers

I have worked on the Tweed's Bemersyde beat for nearly 32 years and have witnessed a serious decline in fish numbers. From September onwards, the fish "run" i.e. go up the river from the sea to spawn, but there are far fewer fish coming into the river: last year 63 fish were caught on our beat compared to around 200 five years ago. In September and October, the numbers being caught plummeted. On one day in October 2018 I did not see a single fish in the river. My personal opinion is that catch-and-release rules should be extended to include September, October and November for the immediate future.

Predators

It is more difficult to control global environmental and global factors, but we can take action on our own rivers to mitigate the decline: while fish numbers have been falling, the numbers of predators, notably goosanders and cormorants have increased considerably. When I first started working here, goosanders and cormorants were a rarity: indeed, birdwatchers came here in the hope of glimpsing one. Now I see as many as 30 in a day, openly predating the fish, not just salmon but parr, trout and small trout too. Cormorant numbers have increased in the past five or six years – there is a roost at Rutherford with up to 100 birds - and you can easily watch them eating the fish too. The huge seal population on the coast and the number of seals coming up the river is also not helping.

The bird populations are of course important, but in balance and in their natural habitat. The goosander numbers are too high and the cormorants – ordinarily a sea bird - are an alien species so far up the Tweed. We have recently been licenced to shoot a limited number of goosanders to send away and test to see what is in their stomachs. We are also tagging smolts (juvenile salmon) and heading back to sea from April to June – to see what is eating them. Around 60% of smolts don't reach the sea: most are eaten by goosander and cormorants.

• ACTION: Goosander, cormorant and seal numbers need to be reduced and controlled.

Man-Made Impediments

When the woollen tweed industry was established on the river a series of caulds (weirs or dams which directed water to the mill-lades) were built. Some of these remain and if the water is cold, the fish can stop behind them.

• ACTION: Man-made impediments should be removed so that the river can return to its natural flow and fish can move more easily through the water.

Low water on Tweed at Mertoun Cauld

Courtesy: Ian Farr, Bemersyde

The Tweed

People come from all over the world, especially Belgium, Germany, Norway and Sweden, as well as the rest of the UK to fish on the Tweed. They come for the sport and the ambience of Scotland, which they see as the birthplace of salmon fishing. The Tay, Spey, Dee and Tweed are believed to be the best salmon rivers and are the most famous in the world. We are starting to lose that prowess.

Effect On Tourism/Local Economy

The decline in fish numbers is already affecting local economies. Tourists used to come wondering how many fish they would catch, now they wonder if they will catch even one. People who previously booked fishing here year in and year out, are holding off to see if there are any fish coming into the system before making a reservation. This is not just happening on the Tweed but all over Scotland. On Monday this week there were around 5-600 people on Scotland's four major rivers, but they only caught 20 fish between them.

Scotland's salmon rivers, by their nature, run deep into our rural communities. There are around 30 beats on the Tweed: most have a full-time ghillie, some have three or four and normally employ extra ghillies at the back-end. Last year, we did not employ people on this basis, only by the day as required. Our bookings are down by 60 per cent compared to five years ago. Usually we offer six rods a day but by last November we had no bookings at all and our income has halved. People who come here to fish stay in local hotels and B&Bs; they buy their tackle, waders and flies from the tackle shop, their sandwich from the local bakery or petrol station.

The Future

I seriously fear that this could be the last generation of salmon fishing in Scotland and the last generation of full-time ghillies. We are running a business here and we have to cover our costs. Ghillies build their experience of their beat over many years. Every fish caught goes into the memory bank but there will be no incentive for people to learn how to fish if there are no fish to be caught. The fly-tiers, wader and rod manufacturers are not going to sell kit. The whole industry could just wither away. At Bemersyde we plan to build a trout pond. Fishing from a pond will provide some recreation but the experience is completely different."

Scottish Government response

In September 2019, the Scottish Government published a policy document: *Protecting Scotland's Future: the Government's programme for Scotland 2019-2020.* This contained a number of commitments - to the natural environment and biodiversity; to rural land-use, forestry, peatlands and tourism. All of those commitments can have collateral benefits for wild salmon and salmon fishing. But, most importantly, the programme includes a commitment to publish a "multi−year national wild Atlantic salmon strategy " by September 2020.

This is a long-awaited and much-needed commitment. Its success will depend very much on the quality of the information gathered to inform such a strategy and ensuring that this is of the necessary standard. This will require significant government investment as resources from the levy on the salmon fisheries are falling.

CHAPTER 6

Salmon In Crisis?
What do the Data Suggest?

The evidence of a species in crisis appears undeniable. In the 1970s some 15-25% of the smolts, sent out to sea, returned as grilse or adult fish. In 2017 that percentage had declined to 4%. On 19 August 2019, the Scottish Parliament received a Briefing Paper on *"Wild Salmon"*. Starting with the acknowledgement that:

> "Wild salmon in Scotland are in decline, having reached their lowest rod catch ever in 2018. Salmon face a number of different pressures as they migrate from their spawning grounds in rivers down to the coast, across the open ocean and back to their native rivers again."

The Briefing Paper provides a comprehensive and detailed review of the importance, status, threats and opportunities for conserving Scotland's king of fish. Within the overall catch statistics, spring salmon have generally declined and although there is some indication that catches have stabilised in recent years, they remain at a low level. Catches of salmon and grilse in later months, on the other hand, generally increased up to 2010, after which they fell sharply over the next 4 years before recovering slightly in 2015 and 2016 only to fall again in 2017 and 2018.

Limitations of catch-returns

The catch records, as they are currently collected, only show the numbers of fish caught. They do not take into account the number of fishing-days required to catch the fish or the river conditions that may have affected angling-success. Any combination of lack of fish, lack of water or reports of poor angling-success can discourage anglers from coming to fish the river at all. Data on angling effort for rod-and-line fisheries is being collected from 2019.

Some qualification may be required on the definition of some of the words used in the motion for the 19 April debate in the Scottish Parliament . What do the words - 'long-term' and 'persistent decline' - actually mean in relation to the observed rod catches. While there is evidence that the Scottish salmon rod-and-line catches have 'declined' over recent years, the rate and distribution of the decline is variable. Some rivers are affected more than others. Tweed, for example produced excellent catches in 2010 and 2011, believed to be due to good smolt survival in 2009.

The motion for the April 19 debate refers to salmon 'stocks' - but there are a number of separate 'stocks' or components of stocks. Bearing in mind the genetic differentiation of salmon from, and within, different rivers, there could be said to be a multiplicity of different 'stocks' of salmon. At a basic level, the headline figures for salmon rod-catches do not differentiate between grilse, which return after one winter at sea, and salmon, which spend two or more winters at sea. These components of the stock have different feeding patterns at sea and therefore suffer different impacts from the changing ocean climate. The headline figures also do not show the seasonality of the returning salmon. There is evidence that grilse are returning to some Scottish rivers earlier than in the past and there is strong evidence to show a cyclical change in return timing, of both grilse and salmon, between spring, summer and autumn seasons. The data behind the headline figure for Scottish rod-catches in 2018 reveal a much more complex and dynamic situation than the headline figures suggest.

Dr Ronald Campbell, Senior Biologist of The Tweed Foundation, provides the rod catch figures for the Tweed from 1970 until 2018. These show that the ten-year period, 2003-13, was a time of particularly good catches, and therefore a stark contrast with the present. The present contrast with the 1990s is less stark, when 8-10,000 salmon a year was "normal". As recently as 2010, the River Tweed caught it highest-ever rod catch. The period from 2003 to 2013 was a period of exceptional catches generally and it would be useful to know what was different about this period, which appeared to be good in other rivers.

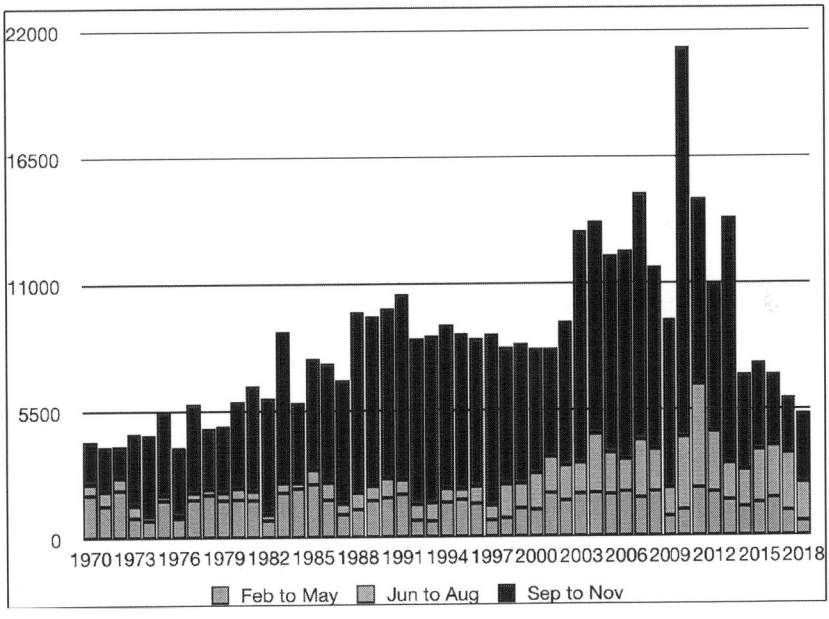

Tweed rod-catches: 1970-2018

Courtesy: The Tweed Foundation

Again, Campbell, refers to the Tweed. "The population of salmon in the river has not declined, there are as many juveniles as ever in the nursery streams. What has declined has been the number of adults returning from the sea and, in particular, the number of grilse. Numbers of multi-sea winter salmon are remaining much the same. The graph suggests there has been no long-term decline in the spring and summer totals of the Tweed, except in the bad years of 2009 and 2018. The recent decline in catches has been due to the decline in grilse, particularly late in the season. This situation has arisen before in the historical record."

Catches versus Stocks

Angling catches can only be an indirect reflection of the available stocks of fish. Many salmon only enter the river after the angling season is finished so are never reflected in the angling catch although some of this data is obtained by fish-counters upstream. Some Fishery Boards operate hatcheries and release juvenile salmon into the river systems. The contribution of hatchery-reared salmon to the angling catch is uncertain but may confuse the status of wild stocks.

The net upstream salmon count for 2018 at Pitlochry Dam (2682), albeit a river modified by hydro-electric generation, was the second lowest ever. The main cause of the low overall count, was very poor summer and autumn counts, suggesting another poor run of grilse.

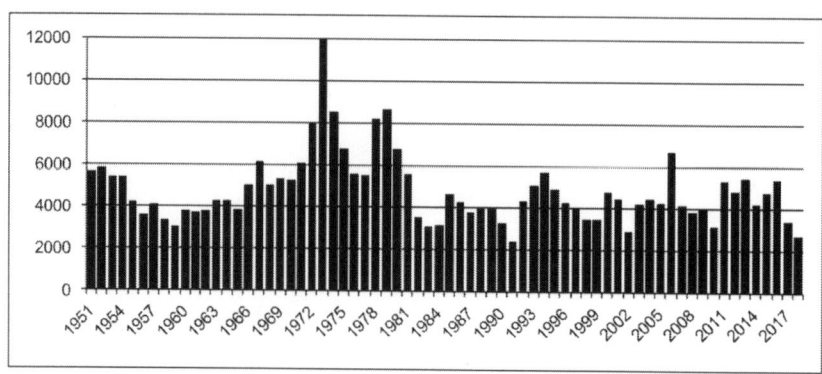

Annual net upstream counts through Pitlochry Dam, 1951-2018.

Courtesy: SSE

Where have all the salmon gone?

The mantra of 'lost at sea' reverberates around the conservation world - with good reason - but it is not just at sea that the salmon is facing problems. The scientists at Scottish Government's Marine Scotland Science (MSS) have identified a number of 'high-level pressures' which illustrate the wide research into possible solutions to the decline of Scotland's salmon. Regular monitoring of nursery areas in the rivers by electrofishing indicates that juvenile stocks of salmon are very abundant with no consistent signs of decline. In addition the number of rivers accessible for salmon in Scotland has increased, eg the Clyde, Gala and the Almond in the Lothians and the River Garry in Perthshire, all greatly increasing the potential production of smolts.

By the time the juvenile salmon are ready to go to sea as smolts there is a general abundance leaving the nursery streams. Campbell reminds us that "at any one time, 90% of the Atlantic salmon alive in the world are under 120mm in length and living in freshwater. In Scotland, the numbers of these fish have not changed, so stocks are not under any immediate threat. What has changed is the numbers of adults coming back from the sea – and that decline is mainly in the numbers of grilse." Research is on-going to establish what happens to the smolts in their journey to the sea. Further international research is investigating what happens to the salmon when it is migrating and feeding at sea and why only 5% of smolts are returning to Scottish rivers now, compared with 25% in the 1970s.

CHAPTER 7

High Level Pressures
Researching Wild Salmon

Courtesy: River Dee Trust

Marine Scotland Science has identified a number of 'high-level pressures' which guide its salmon research. These include issues of *Exploitation, Predation, Fish Health, Genetic Introgression* and *Invasive Species* which mainly affect the salmon itself - as a fish. Other pressures are felt on the salmon's habitat, the river environment in which we fish, and include issues of *Water Quality, Water Quantity, Water Temperature, In-stream Habitats* and *Riparian Habitats.*

Marine Scotland Science is developing an on-line mapping-based tool to enable individual District Salmon Fishery Boards to understand the severity and status of each of these pressures across their catchment areas. This will provide a national and a local picture to inform future policy thinking. Scientists and managers will be able to identify which lengths of rivers are impacted by each pressure and establish priorities for action.

Exploitation

This major 'high-level stress' includes both legal (nets and rods) and illegal exploitation. The Scottish Government continues to lay Annual Conservation Regulations and to consider extensions to Spring closure periods. Scotland's salmon rivers are categorised, in terms of the sustainability of their salmon stocks, into three grades. Rivers in which the spawning target has less than 60% chance of being achieved are given Grade 3 categorisation and subject to a ban on killing. When the spawning target has a 60% to 80% chance of being achieved, Grade 2 is allocated and killing may continue if measures are put in place locally to increase status. Rivers and stocks with higher conservation status are Grade 1 and killing may occur subject to local control.

The assessment for the 2019 season, i.e. the numbers of eggs required to produce sustainable Atlantic salmon stocks was estimated from an increased number of rivers (11), where information on stock-recruitment relationships and associated data was available. For 2019, the latest assessment showed that the downward trend in salmon stocks was continuing. However, changes and improvements to the assessment mean that properly-managed exploitation could be allowed on a greater number of rivers than in the 2018 season. There was an increase in the number of Grade 1 and Grade 2 rivers for 2019, with fewer rivers being subject to Grade 3 (mandatory catch and release) requirements. This will now be fixed for two years, until the 2022 assessment, within which period it will be fully and transparently peer-reviewed.

Predation and Competition.

At various stages of its life-cycle the salmon suffers from predation or competition by fish-eating birds, other fish, seals, dolphins, otters and other creatures. There are suggestions that the increase in mackerel stocks around parts of the coast have an impact on wild salmon in the sea, perhaps as smolts or post-smolts. A number of projects to track the smolt run on several rivers, to assess losses in relation to sawbill ducks and marine mammals, are described later.

Fish health

Salmon survival can be impacted by disease, sea-lice and other parasites. The Scottish Government's response to the current state of the salmon-farming industry, identified opportunities for its future development and explored how the various fish-health and environmental challenges it currently faces can be addressed.

Sea-lice. There is little doubt that sea-lice, associated with salmon farming in the waters on the west coast and islands, pose the biggest health threat to wild salmon and sea trout. The short, west coast rivers had special stocks with high proportions of repeat-spawning salmon and these have now gone. Marine Science Scotland continues research by sweep-netting at the Shieldaig site to provide data and investigate potential links between post-smolts, sea trout and sea-lice and fish farms.

Dr Alan Wells, Chief Executive of Fisheries Management Scotland, recognises that the impact of sea-lice, the escapes of farmed fish and the lack of coordination between regulators, "are the fundamental issues that needs to be addressed." Wells acknowledges that finfish aquaculture is vital to Scotland's economy, particularly on the west coast. "However", says Wells, "the economic and cultural importance of our wild fish and fisheries should not be overshadowed by this, and we must ensure that the regulation of finfish farms is firmly grounded in the principles of sustainable development." Fisheries Management Scotland is involved with a number of Working Groups and Committees to try to address these problems. Environmental Management Plans may bring forward the issues but Fisheries Management Scotland recognises that reform of the regulatory and planning regime is required. Wells recognises that time is limited. "There is a real urgency", he pleads, "to ensure proper regulation of this important industry – our wild salmon and sea trout deserve no less."

By 2020 the salmon-farming industry aims to sustainably produce 210,000 tonnes of marine finfish, increasing to 350,000 tonnes per year by 2030, an increase of 115 %. The planned expansion of Scottish aquaculture is anticipated to boost its value from £1.8bn in 2016 to £3.6bn by 2030 but the Scottish Rural Economy and Connectivity Committee's report on *Salmon Farming* recognised that "maintaining the status quo in terms of the regulatory regime in Scotland is not an option" and recommends "a comprehensively updated package of regulation both to ensure the sector will be managed effectively and to provide a strong foundation on which it can grow in a sustainable manner". One option is for fish-farms to either move onshore or use solid-wall containers at sea, rather than nets. The answer may depend on how soon we see meaningful advances in "closed containment" or recirculating aquaculture systems. Closed containment production will likely increase but whether it replaces traditional cage-production will depend on economic, political and environment considerations.

There are examples of good aquaculture regulation in Ireland, Denmark and Norway. The Danes are perhaps in the forefront. Environment Minister, Lea Wermelin, said in a recent statement. "Denmark has reached the limit of the number of fish that can be raised at sea without endangering the environment........ We must be a green pioneer, including fish farming." This move means that the government will put an end to developing new aquaculture projects in the country but its 19 existing fish farms will not be affected.

Genetic introgression

There is a risk to wild salmon stocks from the genetic impacts of farmed salmon escaping from fish-farms or from deliberate stocking of salmon with inappropriate genetics. A national introgression project commenced in 2018 seeks to quantify levels of introgression of genetic material from farm escapees into wild Scottish Atlantic salmon populations. A review of the current licensing process which permits salmon introductions (stocking) will be completed in advance of 2020 season.

Invasive non-native species

In the water environment the salmon can be at risk from non-native species such as the American Signal Crayfish and Pacific Pink Salmon while river banks are affected by invasive plant species such as Himalayan Balsam. The Scottish Invasive Species Initiative is a priority project in the Scottish Biodiversity Strategy to 2020.

Other issues of *Water Quality*, *Water Quantity*, *Water Temperature* and *In-stream* and *Riparian Habitats* - are considered in later chapters.

CHAPTER 8

Lost at Sea?
Salmon In A Changing Ocean

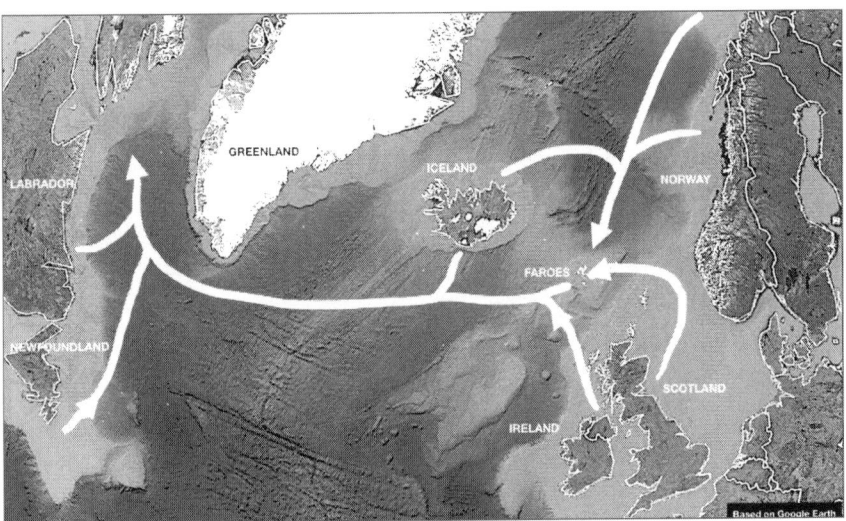

Approximate migration routes in the North Atlantic

In the 1970s some 25% of the young salmon leaving our rivers could expect to return to freshwater. By 2018 the figure had reduced to 5%. Where have all the salmon gone? This question has perplexed scientists for many years.

'Salmon at Sea' - 'The SALSEA Project'

In 2001, in response to decades of declining salmon stocks in the North Atlantic the North Atlantic Salmon Conservation Organization (NASCO) and partners established an International Atlantic Salmon Research Board (IASRB). This led to an international research programme - The Salmon at Sea or SALSEA project in 2005. Over the following years an intensive research programme accumulated a large amount of data to increase understanding of how Atlantic salmon use the ocean; where they go; how they use ocean currents and the ocean's food resources and what factors influence migration and distribution at sea. In 2008, a further collaborative three-year project - SALSEAMerge - created a database of genetic and ecological investigations to shed light on the increased marine mortality. A review of progress was held at a 'Salmon Summit' in 2011.

SALSEA established the concept of an annual "conveyor belt" of northward-migrating smolts. Along this route, the number of smolts declines due to cumulative effects of natural mortality as well as any fishing mortality. In particular, SALSEA identified the existence of "choke points" in the ocean, where there is coalescence of migrating smolts in relatively restricted geographical areas and where there is believed to be potential for variations in oceanic conditions to alter the destinations of migrating smolts. Additional mortality factors likely operate during the overwinter feeding phase and on the return migration to home waters and entry to rivers. A full description of the SALSEA project and its outcomes is described in the '2011 Salmon Summit'.

The 'Missing Salmon Project'

Despite the greater understanding provided by the SALSEA programme, salmon were still being 'lost at sea'. In 2018, to find out where the salmon were being 'lost', the Atlantic Salmon Trust, with partners, formed the Missing Salmon Alliance, to fund 'The Missing Salmon Project'. Based on an established process, 'a suspects framework' was designed to prioritise the factors implicated in the decline of salmon stocks.

The 'Likely Suspects Framework' tries to identify - 'where?' and 'how much? '- salmon mortality takes place and how those factors have changed between periods of higher marine survival of 25% in the 1970s and the more current low survival phase of only 5%. It covers the freshwater migration phase and the marine phase with the overall objective of quantifying the potential of each "likely suspect" to influence survival. The 'likely suspects' include: - over-fishing; habitat destruction; barriers; drop in water quality; increase in predators; aquaculture; warming oceans and warming freshwaters. The overall framework covers both the freshwater migration and the marine phases of the salmon's life cycle and forms an evidence base to support management plans at local, national and international levels. In 2019 The Atlantic Salmon Trust published a 'Blue Book' - *Atlantic salmon mortality at sea: Developing an evidence-based "Likely Suspects" Framework.*

Key geographical areas and periods where mortality factors are known, or thought, to operate are characterised as ecosystem 'domains', which can be identified at various locations, ranging from freshwater to marine feeding areas. These 'domains' are associated with different mortality factors which may impact many stocks, a few stocks or even just a single stock. Salmon from any given stock pass through successive mortality 'domains', on their migratory journey. Some domains can be identified as: parr to smolt transformation; smolt migration from freshwater and through estuaries; estuary/sea interface and early marine life (coastal/near shore); migration pathways to oceanic feeding grounds; overwintering/feeding areas; return migration and entry to home waters and home river.

In the marine phase mortality factors can operate cumulatively as salmon pass through various ecosystem 'domains'. Some factors become critical in years of bad oceanic conditions, but matter less in good years. In bad years the smaller salmon get eaten! It is important to concentrate on the places and times where mortality is likely to affect a large number of stocks. Major areas of interest are not necessarily at oceanic scale but could include discreet 'hotspots' in freshwater, estuary or early marine phase, where smolts get slowed down and get preyed upon.

In 2018, Professor Ken Whelan, on behalf of the Atlantic Salmon Trust, presented a paper to the North Atlantic Salmon Summit in Iceland on how the 'Suspects Framework' can be used for - *Integrating the Approaches and Managing the Challenges'* - in conserving salmon at sea. Using the methodology, of the 'Likely Suspects Framework' he presented a balance sheet of how many salmon have been lost from UK stocks and where they are being lost.

By comparing the average Pre-Fishery Abundance between 1971 and 1975 (1,061,000) with the average Pre-Fishery Abundance between 2012 and 2016 (495,000), there is a loss of 566,000 salmon to account for. The Likely Suspects Framework study estimated that this mortality was shared between the domains of :

- Nearshore: Estuarine, Coastal, Homewater   244,000
- Conveyor Belt   266,000
- Pelagic by-catch   56,000

Therefore, if 'Nearshore' and 'Pelagic' losses were tackled, this would account for 53% of the total losses in the domains of the marine "suspects".

These large-scale climatic effects do not just affect the salmon at sea but also the freshwater phase of its life-cycle. In his Chairman's Summary at the Salmon Summit in 2011, Paul Knight emphasised that: -

"Although SALSEA looked primarily at marine issues, it is important to remember that mortality occurs during all of the salmon's life stages, and so the freshwater phase cannot be divorced from the marine. This is especially important in the face of climate change, whose potential impact looms over most of the issues affecting Atlantic salmon, but especially those in freshwater, estuarine and coastal areas. Water temperatures in the salmon's southern range may rise by up to 7°C over the coming century, and the ability of the species to survive the inevitable environmental change will be critical in this region."

The Moray Firth Tracking Project

One of the gaps identified in the knowledge of 'Nearshore' losses in the 'Missing Salmon Project' was the fate of smolts as they migrated downstream and out to sea. The Atlantic Salmon Trust is currently coordinating a tracking project in the Moray Firth, which is described Chapter 10.

CHAPTER 9

Looking After the Juveniles
The Changing Nursery Streams

"We should manage what we are best able to manage - especially in the freshwater, estuarine and coastal zones. In particular, salmon managers should make their main objective to maximise production and output to the marine environment of high quality smolts, with particular attention to growth, survival, migration timing and interaction with other species, both prey and predator."

Paul Knight, Salmon Summit, 2011

The nursery streams which produce the smolts are also affected by climatic changes. Freshwater practices affect the number and quality of juvenile salmon sent to sea and influence their subsequent survival. These can be population-specific or broader in impact and managers need to understand what is happening at sea to make sense of the impact of freshwater decisions. Three particular aspects of change which can influence the smolt production from the nursery streams are: a) opportunities for increasing carrying capacity of these streams; b) replacing lost nutrients; c) increasing water temperatures and the need to keep the water cool.

Increasing carrying capacity - Providing more useable space

Establishing riparian woodland and restoring the in-stream habitat are seen as key elements for increasing the numbers of fit, healthy smolts these streams produce each year. Recent studies have shown that fitter smolts have a much higher chance of surviving at sea and returning as adults.

The survival of young salmon is density-dependent. A relatively small number of returning adults can fully populate a nursery stream and fulfil its 'carrying capacity' for smolts. However, there are opportunities to increase the carrying capacity of those upland streams. Changes to the physical shape of the river and its bed can increase the space, shelter and food for young salmon and provide deeper, cooler refuges. Flow restrictors can encourage out-of-bank flow and hold back water, thus "slowing the flow", while engineered log jams or large woody debris can be created from local timber and deployed in a number of different ways.

Dr Hamish Moir, Managing Director of Cbec Eco-engineering UK Ltd, has been involved in three such major projects on the Gairn, the Nairn and the Allt Lorgy tributary of the Dulnain - all aimed at improving the channel diversity of these upland streams to increase their carrying capacity for parr and smolts.

In the headwaters of the Nairn, from 2014 to 2017, the company carried out a catchment-scale restoration on a river which had historically been straightened, dredged and embanked. The restoration aimed at reinstating natural physical processes and involved the realignment of 1.5 km of channel; adding more than 7000 cubic metres of gravel; installing 18 large wood structures; removing more than 2.5 km of embankment and creating three 'online' wetland areas. The development of the wetland areas is particularly important, since they represent ecological 'hotpots' and are largely absent in a UK context. Post-project surveys reveal rapid channel adjustment towards increased complexity, especially close to large wood structures and existing biological data - invertebrate samples, electro-fishing surveys, redd counts - provide a baseline for measuring the ecological response to the scheme.

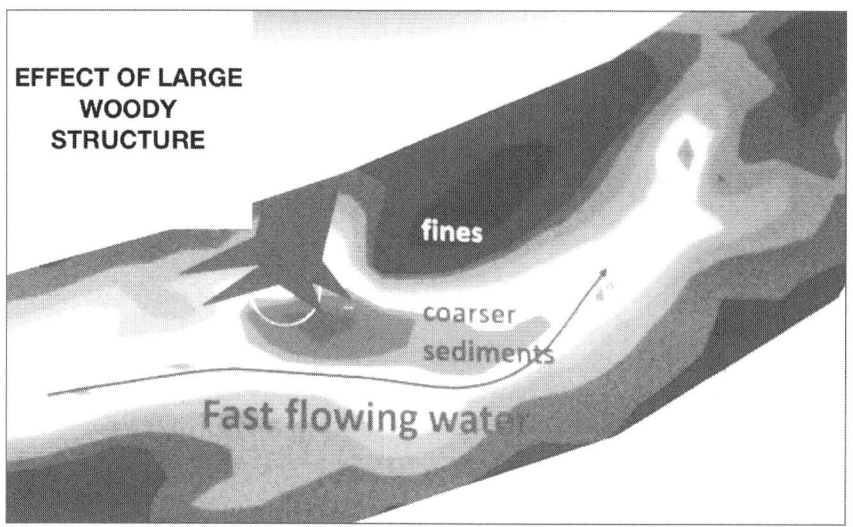

Effect of 'large woody structure' (tree root) on stream morphology
Courtesy: Cbec Eco-engineering UK

The Gairn is a large upland tributary of the River Dee, Aberdeenshire. Historically exhibiting old growth forest cover, the River Gairn catchment was deforested some centuries ago. The loss of large wood input to the channel resulted in a generally homogenous 'plane bed' channel morphology with coarse substrate and relatively little provision of salmonid spawning habitat. In association with the Dee District Salmon Fishery Board and the River Dee Trust, large wood structures were installed over a 6 km length of the river to enhance geomorphic processes and sediment transport to encourage a more natural and diverse channel with associated ecological benefits.

Edwin Third, Operations Manager of the Dee District Salmon Fishery Board, represented the Dee District Salmon Fishery Board on the Gairn project and describes some of the issues affecting the Dee headwaters and their innovative solutions:

"Practically all of Scotland's upland rivers would have once flowed through extensive areas of woodland, which helped to create ideal habitat for salmon, by regulating temperature and flows and by providing shade and nutrients. Trees falling into the river created pools, spawning gravels, cover and a range of flow conditions which suited the complex habitat requirements of all life stages of salmon. They also supported higher numbers of invertebrates by trapping nutrients for key species groups, such as mayflies, stoneflies and caddisflies. However, deforestation of our upland streams has resulted in the rivers becoming around 30 percent wider and shallower. Rivers like the Gairn often now reach peak summer water temperatures of over 20°C and in 2018 reached 27.5°C (81.5°F), very close to the lethal limit for juvenile salmon. "

The newly planted trees in the Dee catchment will take decades before they grow large enough to fall into the river and create the habitat improvements that salmon require. In order to kick-start the process the Board created large woody structures during 2018 and 2019. Over 170 large wind-blown Scots pine trees were transported to the upper Gairn from the nearest woodland, around eight miles away. These were then securely dug into the bank or bed of the river to mimic natural woody structures and located where they would create narrowing and speeding up of the stream.

Replacing lost nutrients - Improving the food supply

With the reducing number of salmon returning to their spawning streams, there is evidence that such streams and their populations of juvenile salmon are losing out in an important source of nutrients. A substantial supply of nutrients would naturally come from decaying salmon carcasses during the winter spawning season. Streams that lack dead adult salmon support fewer insects, and therefore produce less food, so that the surviving salmon fry are smaller and belong to fewer families. The resulting loss of genetic diversity could make these salmon populations more vulnerable to extinction.

The late Simon Mckelvey, explored the importance of salmon carcasses and other sources of nutrients in the Conon catchment. He also noted that human activity could also lead to oligotrophication in the middle and upper catchments and that this was commonplace over much of north and northwest Scotland. In particular, phosphorus may be lacking from many salmon nursery streams, with returning adults being the only natural source of replacement. Loss of riparian habitat, overgrazing, construction of dams and decline in the numbers of returning salmon dying in headwater streams all contribute to habitats unnaturally devoid of nutrients. The Conon is particularly impacted by all these issues.

Experiments showed that introducing salmon carcasses into streams increased invertebrate densities and isotopes could be used to demonstrate the uptake of marine nutrients by these invertebrates. The numbers of juvenile salmon above and below the salmon carcass addition sites increased in proportion to carcass addition and at some sites doubled. Replacing dead salmon with nutrient pellets in hessian sacks also produced an increase in invertebrates and an increase in salmon growth-rate and biomass. Further work is investigating whether this increase in growth-rate will result in larger smolts and will change the age of 'smolting'.

Keeping the nursery streams cool - providing shade and depth

High water temperatures can be found throughout the river system from the headwaters to the sea. However, it is in the upper tributaries, the main spawning and nursery areas where the effect of increasing temperatures are usually considered to be most significant.

Ronald Campbell refers to the effect of the North Atlantic Oscillation, the switch in high pressure between Iceland and the Azores. A high North Atlantic Oscillation means warmer, more westerly, weather for the British Isles and evidence suggests that, in warmer North Atlantic Oscillations, fry emerge earlier and this extra growth period can affect changes in smolt ages. "There is a check and balance here", he suggests, "even if late summer becomes too warm for parr to grow, they will have more of a growth period earlier on – assuming their prey species also adjust accordingly." If fry emergence becomes earlier this could affect the timing of when parr become smolts.

Campbell also cites evidence that salmon can adapt to changes in both freshwater and marine temperatures. The Tweed shows how smolt ages can vary with temperatures. In 1929 and 1930, only 5% of smolts spent 3 or 4 years in freshwater (S3 and S4). The 1940s, 1950s and 1960s were periods of long, cold winters and shorter growing seasons, so parr grew more slowly and smolts got older, such that by the 1960s, some 60% of smolts were spending 3 or 4 winters in freshwater. In the 2010s, by contrast, 75% of smolts only spend 1 winter in freshwater (S1), which suggests the effect of warming. This is another check and balance. The more smolts leave early at S1, the more habitat becomes available for fry to grow into. In the 1960s, three cohorts of juvenile salmon were sharing out the habitat - fry, 1-year old parr and 2-year old parr. Now there is really only one cohort - the fry - so the available habitat of the catchment is, effectively, now much larger than it was in the 1960s.

Since 2013 the Dee District Salmon Fishery Board and River Dee Trust have planted over 180,000 native trees along the river banks of the upper Dee and its tributaries, including the Geldie, Ey, Gairn, Clunie, Baddoch, Callater, Slugain, Gelder and Muick. This project works with the estates of Mar Lodge, Mar, Invercauld and Balmoral ensuring that areas of riparian woodland do not compromise the primary land management for grouse and deer. In 2019 the Dee received further funding from Scottish Natural Heritage's Biodiversity Challenge Fund which will allow the "10,000 tree" project to continue this restoration. To achieve a significant reduction in summer temperatures and improve upland stream habitat, this work needs to be carried out on a catchment scale.

Projects to keep the water cool are not confined to Scotland. On the other side of the Atlantic, in Canada, Ben Goldfarb reports that:

"Since 2014, the Miramichi Salmon Association has completed nine cold-water restoration projects, using heavy machinery to deepen holes, deflect flows from creek mouths into the main current, and install boulders to make cold pools even more enticing. Smarter forestry management can help, too. Protecting forests in the headwaters of the Miramichi watershed, and leaving broad riparian buffers bracketing streams, slows down runoff after rainstorms, reducing erosion and keeping chilly water in the river longer.......The circumstances for Atlantic salmon may be dire, but they're not hopeless. The Miramichi River is honeycombed with frigid pockets, groundwater-fed seeps and brooks that bubble into the main stem and create pools that remain several degrees colder than the surrounding river. To an angler, these cold spots offer enticing fishing holes. To a salmon, they're life-savers."

CHAPTER 10

Running the Gauntlet
Getting The Smolts To Sea

"In many rivers, juvenile salmon are growing faster and smolts are migrating to sea at a younger age and, typically, smaller sizes. ....Smolt run-timing is also occurring earlier across the geographic range, with increasing concerns that this might result in a mismatch with optimum marine conditions - the environmental "smolt window".

Russell et al: Salmon Summit, 2011

Salmon smolt - The future of salmon stocks

One of the most vulnerable stages in the salmon's life-cycle is the journey of the smolt from nursery stream down to the sea.

As Ben Goldfarb puts it: "Hit the ocean too early or too late and you might miss your prime feeding window, collide with predators, or even struggle to regulate your physiology. Although your departure for the ocean is partly governed by seasonal changes in daylight, temperature also plays a major role. In 2014, researchers found that, as rivers around the North Atlantic have warmed over the past 50 years, smolt migrations have shifted forward by 2.5 days per decade. That may sound subtle, but when you're a hungry, vulnerable smolt, even the slightest mismatch between river and ocean could prove fatal."

From the nursery streams to the sea - tracking the smolts

A number of studies are underway to shed light on the journey to the sea and identify losses along the way. Roger Knight, River Director, Spey District Salmon Fishery Board, highlights some of the work to reduce predation pressure on migratory fish:

"Recent and ongoing studies on the Dee, Tweed and Deveron have suggested that, during the early part of the smolts' journey within the river, these young fish sustain high losses. It is known that some of these losses are down to predation from fish-eating birds – such as goosanders, mergansers and cormorants – and these can be moved off rivers by a variety of means, including shooting to scare. These birds are also protected, so shooting to scare activities take place under a licence issued by Scottish Natural Heritage, which authorises these activities to take place both prior to, and during, the downstream smolt migration.

In order to better understand the impact of fish-eating birds and to support applications to Scottish Natural Heritage, some District Salmon Fishery Boards, including the Spey, undertake extensive bird counts throughout the year. These surveys require significant resource and investment, but they enable much of the main river to be surveyed from canoes. In due course, we hope to expand this to the tributaries as well. This work suggests that, at least on some rivers and notably the Spey, the counts of fish-eating birds are increasing significantly. It should also be recognised that many other District Salmon Fishery Boards simply do not have the resources to undertake such work."

For several years, District Salmon Fishery Boards around the Moray Firth have adopted a regional approach to this work and submitted a combined application to Scottish Natural Heritage. More recently, these Moray Firth Boards have been joined by a number of other Scottish rivers to discuss the problem of predation from a more national perspective. In this respect, they have also been joined by Fisheries Management Scotland, Scottish Natural Heritage, Marine Scotland (both Policy and Science), the Centre for Ecology and Hydrology (CEH) and Science and Advice for Scottish Agriculture (SASA).

Additionally, Fisheries Management Scotland is working with the Scottish Environment Protection Agency and other regulators to ensure that activities and structures licensed in or near our rivers do not expose migratory fish to greater predation risk. For example, dams and weirs can result in migration 'pinch points', where fish accumulate and are therefore easily targeted by fish-eating birds.

Knight further describes the impact of seals on salmon:

> "Like fish-eating birds, both common/harbour seals and grey seals are protected species. Scotland-wide, the population of common seals is declining, whereas the grey seal population is increasing. Work undertaken in the Moray Firth, in partnership with the Sea Mammal Research Unit, demonstrated that a small number of seals develop specialist behaviour, breaking away from the main seal colonies and penetrating well into rivers to feed on salmon and sea trout. While these may only form a small proportion of overall seal populations, they can have a significant and disproportionate impact on migrating and spawning fish."

The River Dee Trust has been studying smolt migration in the river and Aberdeen harbour since 2016. The first year was a pilot study but, in 2017, 101 smolts from the upper and lower Dee catchment were tagged and tracked. Mortality was high - 70% - for smolts from the upper catchment, and lower, but still significant - 13% - for smolts from the lower catchment. Total in-river and estuarine mortality is estimated as 48%, an overall mortality rate of 0.45% per km migrated. It is thought that mortality was due to predation. Smolt losses occurred in the middle and the lower river, where predator densities are greatest. Tagged fish were surviving for, on average, 12 days after they were tagged, suggesting that tagging/handling was not the direct cause of mortality. Smolts from the upper catchment typically spent 20 days migrating through the river to the harbour, whilst it took smolts from the lower catchment less than one day. Because smolts from the upper river spent longer in the main stem Dee, they were vulnerable to in-river predation for substantially longer than smolts produced in the lower catchment.

In 2018, 100 smolts were tagged and 83 were recorded after tagging. In-river tag losses were 21% over approximately 73 miles of river compared with 2017 when 70% were lost over the same distance. In contrast to 2017, tag losses in 2018 were higher in the harbour, where 28% tagged fish were lost over a distance of approximately 1.5 miles, compared to zero losses in 2017. Detections and migration speed were linked to river flows, with increased detections when river levels are high. Smolts tended to be predominantly active during the night with movements mostly occurring between 6 hours before and after midnight. The swimming speed was generally between 0-5 km/hr in the river but became highly variable in the harbour. Swimming speed was positively related to river flow and the day of the year, indicating that smolts swim faster when river flows are higher and also swim faster as the season progresses. Additionally, swimming speeds are higher during the night. This led to smolts passing through the harbour between 13th April and 15th May. The consistent pattern of increased smolt movements in relation to river flows, the predominantly nocturnal activity patterns and the relationship between swimming speed and discharge and day of the year, have clear implications for the way the smolt migration is managed.

Marine mammal predation

As part of the Dee smolt project, the Seals and Salmon Interaction's work at the Sea Mammal Research Unit will conclude their analysis of photo-identification and behavioural observation data by March 2020. This will inform the number of seals using the Dee system and provide estimates of potential salmon removals from the Dee by seals. Surface cameras will be installed to trial their ability to record seal movements both upstream and downstream in the River Dee.

Fisheries Management Scotland is also working to understand the impact of seal predation on migratory fish, particularly where returning salmon and sea trout need to pass through pinch points where seals accumulate. Preventing or discouraging such seals from entering rivers is the preferred solution, but experience of using a range of acoustic deterrent devices has so far shown them to almost never be completely effective. There is an urgent need to develop improved, fully effective technological solutions to deter seals from entering rivers. It is also important that fisheries managers have the ability to remove problem seals from within rivers. Fisheries Management Scotland is exploring the feasibility of relocating such seals to less sensitive places, but in some limited circumstances, licensed removal of seals may be necessary.

Fisheries Management Scotland recognises that predation is a sensitive and controversial subject and that these birds and seals are also protected species. There has to be a balance, though, and a recognition of the impact that these predators are having on other species such as Atlantic salmon, which are now under significant threat. Fisheries Management Scotland works within the existing legal framework to conserve and protect these native fish. A joint research project between Marine Scotland, the Ness District Salmon Fishery Board and Aberdeen University to identify the impact of dolphin predation on returning adult salmon in the Moray Firth, commenced in 2018 and acoustically-tagged 109 adult grilse.

The Moray Firth Tracking Project

One of the gaps identified in the knowledge of 'Nearshore' losses in the 'Missing Salmon Project' was the fate of smolts as they migrated downstream and out to sea. The Atlantic Salmon Trust is currently coordinating a project in the Moray Firth, where smolts from seven rivers are being tracked from the nursery streams until they leave the firth on the first stage of their ocean journey.

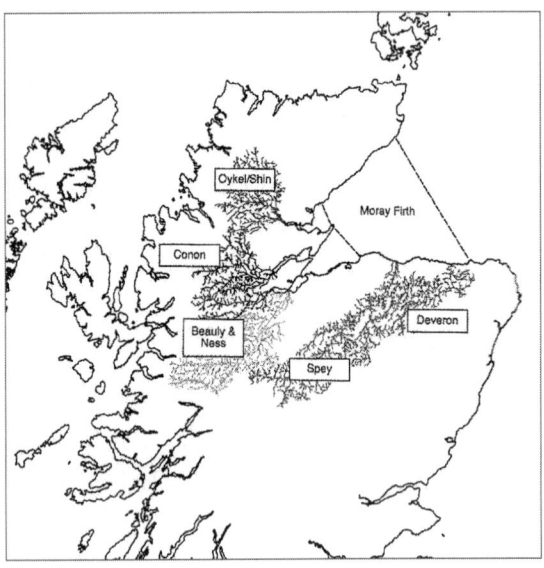

The Moray Firth Tracking Project: Tracking smolts from seven rivers, through the arrays of receivers, out to sea.

Courtesy: Atlantic Salmon Trust

This is the largest acoustic tracking project for salmon in Europe and tracks salmon smolts further than ever before. The lessons learned from the study in the Moray Firth will provide valuable insights that are transferable to other populations of salmon around the UK. Some 800 juvenile salmon are being followed with receivers tracking the smolts' journey to understand where mortality occurs. Analysis of the data is ongoing at the University of Glasgow with preliminary results expected in early 2020.

CHAPTER 11

Homing
Coping with a Changing River

"Tweed catches were low, partly due to low stocks of salmon but also due to climatic and river conditions. Heavy snowfall and blizzards, due to "The Beast from the East", came at the end of February resulting in high waters throughout March. In April, the weather warmed up and continued to do so resulting in a prolonged and hot late Spring, and a sweltering Summer, giving no incentive for fish to move higher up the system due to lack of water.

The River Tweed Commissioners, 2018

The recent concerns are not just about how the salmon itself is affected by climate change but also how it affects our rivers, our sport and the tourist economy of fragile rural parts of Scotland. Changes in climate, alter the pattern of water flows in our rivers and ultimately affect the movement of salmon within the river and the suitability of the river for fishing on any day. If there are no salmon and no water there are no anglers and no income for those who depend upon the salmon fishing.

Scotland has a moist temperate climate with a high average rainfall compared with the rest of the United Kingdom. The country has over 6,000 rivers and a total river network length of in excess of 10,000km. High rainfall levels, low levels of evapotranspiration and the predominance of soil types which limit soil infiltration mean that runoff in Scotland is generally high with many catchments exhibiting flashy responses to rainfall, particularly in areas that are steep. This also means that river flows in many of Scotland's rivers are often high relative to the size of the catchment. There is a perception that river level fluctuations are becoming more extreme and that the extremes are becoming more frequent and lasting longer.

Un-fishable salmon rivers

Un-fishable rivers are not unknown in Scotland. As far back as 1513, one Gavin Douglas could record that: *"Riveris ran reid on spate with water broun, And burnis hurlis all their bankis doun."* There are records of floods on the Eddleston tributary of Tweed in 1839, 1875, 1876, 1881, while a flood of 1832 brought down Eddleston Bridge with fatal results.

There is a perception that the frequency of days when the rivers are un-fishable is increasing. As in the Tweed, 2018 was characterised by long periods of low water in many rivers - not encouraging salmon to migrate upriver nor encouraging them to take a fly when they were in the river. Rain, when it does come, arrives in more intense and localised events with heavy rainfall over a small area. This produces sudden and dirty spates and floods, once again making the river un-fishable - or the fish unresponsive. Even if the river is not in spate nor below summer level, if the river is rising or falling, the fish can be unsettled. Climate change has already resulted in significant changes in rainfall patterns and river flow in Scotland, with further changes predicted over the coming decades. Increasing rainfall intensity, frequency of storms and droughts all affect the stability of our salmon rivers and the opportunities for serious angling.

The Dee, 'bank-high' at Aboyne

Brian Davidson, Director of Communications and Administration, at Fisheries Management Scotland, summarises his concerns in the Annual Report for 2018.

"......2018 was a very challenging season. The winter was cold, while the early spring suffered from the 'Beast from the East'. The remainder of the year was defined by the long and very hot summer, creating not only problems for fisheries and angling, but also for fish survival in some systems. Many rivers reported catches below their five-year averages, with some reporting the lowest catches since the 1950s.

While there are obviously conservation concerns for Atlantic salmon populations as a whole, the extraordinarily dry and hot weather conditions clearly had a profound influence on angling effort and catches. During July, daytime river temperatures in some areas exceeded 19°C, with 27.5°C recorded in the upper Dee catchment, which is close to the lethal limit for salmonids. As a result, fishing effort was low, and even non-existent on some systems, with some proprietors closing fishing due to the extraordinary conditions.

Quite a few rivers managed to regain some lost ground when the rains arrived in the autumn. The later part of season did prove relatively productive, with some rivers reporting the vast majority of their catch in the final two months of their seasons."

Successful salmon angling requires at least two distinct aspects to consider. The first is the presence of fish. The second is 'fishable' river conditions - neither too high nor too low, too hot or too dirty. So how can we manage our rivers and their catchments to reduce the frequency of floods and spates and postpone the onset of low water conditions. Three aspects of changing rivers can be considered - the quality of the water, the quantity of water and the temperature of the water.

Changing Water Quality

Scotland's salmon rivers have been and, to some extent still are, affected by a number of water quality issues - including acidification, point-source pollution, diffuse pollution and eutrophication. Water quality can also be affected by changing rainfall patterns associated with climate change. The European Union Water Framework Directive of 2000 and the impact of recent major floods on farmland and property has shifted public policy in the direction of our rivers.

At a national level, the Water Framework Directive aims for "the protection of inland surface waters, transitional waters, coastal waters and groundwater", from source to sea, preventing the "further deterioration" and protecting and enhancing "the status of aquatic ecosystems". The most important objective within the Water Framework Directive is to achieve a 'good ecological status' for all waters, originally, by 2015. The Directive also considers 'Heavily Modified Water Bodies' (a water body resulted from physical alterations by human activity, which substantially change its character) which are assessed in terms of 'Good Ecological Potential'. The Water Framework Directive enshrines 'river basin management' in United Kingdom legislation, taking account of the whole of a river system to achieve the status of "good ecological quality" for its parts. Scotland is managed as two main catchments - Scotland and Tweed/Solway - with multiple sub-catchments within them. Current river basin management plans have targets for 2021 and 2027.

Much of the water environment in Scotland is in good condition. However, there are still significant problems affecting water quality, physical condition, water flows and levels, and the migration of wild fish. Invasive non-native species are also damaging aquatic plant and animal communities. Water bodies are classified into categories ranging between Bad to High. In 2017, 10% of waters in Scotland reached High category; 46% were assessed as Good and 43.9% were considered to be Less Than Good. The river basin management plans are produced every six years and cover actions for all responsible authorities in Scotland. Consultation took place in 2018 for the Third Phase river basin management plans for publication in 2021. This will include a description of the current condition of the water environment and an assessment of the progress towards achieving the improvement targets set for 2021 and the identification of significant water management challenges.

Changing Water Quantity

Salmon rely on adequate water flows at the right time of year to complete their life-cycle. This can be affected by abstraction, flow regulation, upland land-use and drainage. These can all be exaggerated by changing rainfall patterns as a result of climate change. Marine Scotland Science has undertaken significant research to improve understanding of the effects of flow regime on Atlantic salmon. Scottish Environment Protection Agency has put in place a programme of work to ensure that fish-passage is provided by major operators such as Scottish and Southern Energy and Scottish Water. Scottish Water is investing, in the current investment programme 2015-21, to improve abstraction regimes in nine water resource zones to ensure that there is sufficient water remaining in the water bodies during periods of low rainfall.

Too Much Water

Scotland's temperatures show a recent and rapid warming trend with average spring, summer and winter temperatures having risen by more than 1 degree C since 1961. This has resulted in an increase in precipitation in some parts of the country. Winter precipitation, for example, has increased by almost 60% in the north and west between 1961 and 2004, including the catchments of the Teith, 91%; Nith 69%; Tay 64%; Tweed 63%; Dee 38%, while the Ewe in Wester Ross and the Avon tributary of the Spey show no increase at all. The period of snow cover has shown a decrease over the last 40 years, with early and rapid snowmelt increasing flood risk. While the precise effects of climate change are difficult to predict evidence already exists for increases to river flows in some parts of the country of around 30% between 1961 and 2005 especially for rivers rising in the west, such as the Nith, Tay and Teith. Winter river flows, in particular, have seen a substantial increase in some rivers, corresponding with changes in precipitation.

With the forecast of wetter winters and more intensive rainfall events, further flooding is an increasing risk. Under the Flood Risk Management (Scotland) Act 2009, Scottish Environmental Protection Agency has produced Flood Risk Management Strategies which identify areas of the river catchments as Potentially Vulnerable Areas (PVA) for flooding. In the Tweed catchment, for example, 13 Potentially Vulnerable Areas have been identified. One, covers the valleys of part of the upper River Tweed and its tributaries, the Eddleston Water, Leithen Water, Yarrow Water, Ettrick Water and Gala Water. Since 1977 significant floods have been recorded in this area in 1984, 2003, 2004, 2005, 2009, 2012, and 2013.

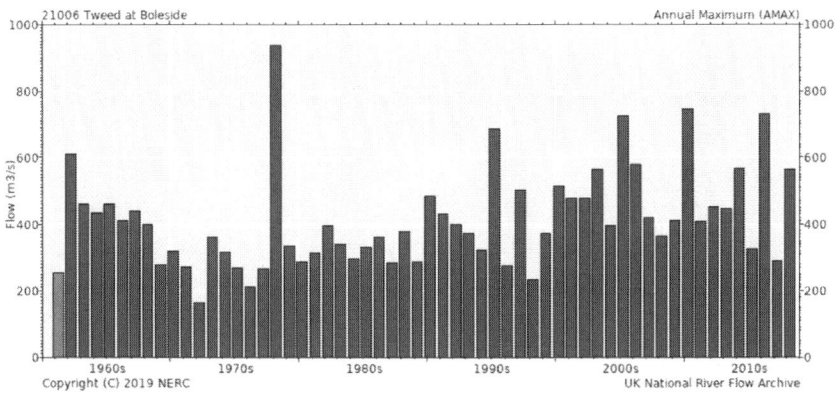

Flood peaks on the Tweed at Boleside since the 1960s
Data from the UK National River Flow Archive

Note: The graph represents the series of maximum instantaneous peak flows within a given water year (October to September) from 1960-2018.

In 2019 the Scottish Government reiterated its commitment to invest £42 million each year for flood protection measures, in addition to funding flood warning and forecasting systems and working on the resilience of our water supply, transport, health services, natural environment, forestry, peatlands and agriculture.

Too little water

Although generally considered a wet country, Scotland can be vulnerable to periods of dry weather. In some areas this can result in pressure on water users and the environment. Climate change is likely to increase uncertainty and may cause issues in areas that have not previously experienced water scarcity. The Scottish Environment Protection Agency produces regular Water Scarcity Situation Reports and provides a link to its Drought Risk Assessment Tool, which shows catchments where rivers are currently at very low flow.

In 2018, Scottish rivers experienced unusually high temperatures and low-flow conditions. As a result, fourteen rivers were defined as having flows below the normal '30-year baseline flow' (1981-2010), including eight rivers rated as suffering 'exceptionally low flows'. Tweed had only 52% of its '30-year baseline flow', the Dee had only 39% and one river in the north of Scotland had only 19% of its average baseline flow. Records show that 69% of rivers experienced thermal stress conditions although none exceeded the temperature that would be lethal for salmon. As a result of climate change recent predictions suggest that, by 2050, there would be a 50% chance of having summers as warm as 2018.

Richard Wright, Bailiff on the River Naver, describes the 2018 season:

"The season started well, although after the end of April things began to take a downturn, with no more significant rises in the river level until the second week in September and the marker gauge at Rhifail measuring -11 inches at our driest. High temperatures were our main concern this season, but we managed to escape without any major fish mortalities. On the six beats anglers refrained from fishing for the majority of July and August, with only four fish being landed in July and none in August, which must be a first for the Naver. Despite this, a fair number of salmon were recorded for the catchment, yet this was still the lowest number since 2003. Good numbers of fish were seen creating redds, although spawning was very stop/start due to the lack of frosts to bring fish on to the redds."

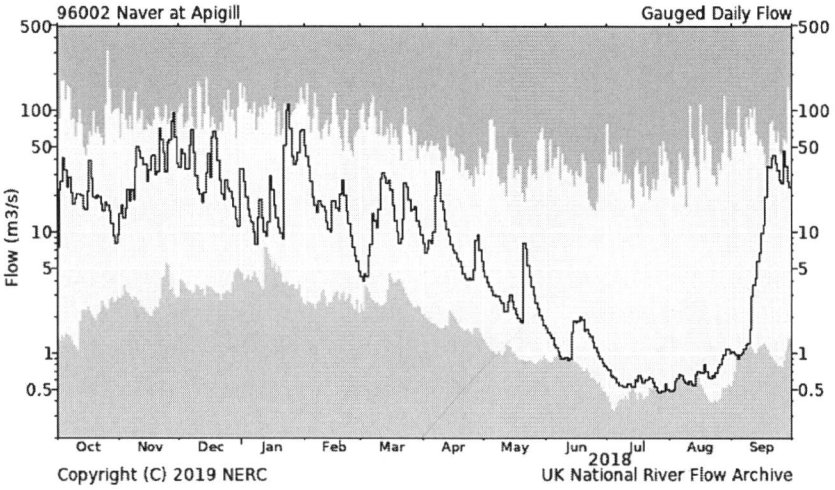

River Naver - Low flows in Summer 2018
Data from the UK National River Flow Archive

While all impoundments have negative effects for migratory salmon, they have some benefits under drought conditions. All Scotland's dams - hydro-electric or water supply - are obliged to release a minimum 'base' or 'compensation' flow to maintain the quality of the river downstream. This ensures that the river ecology is, largely, protected. Many dams also have arrangements to release 'freshets' of water when required. An agreement between the Scottish Environment Protection Agency, the River Tweed Commissioners and Scottish Water allow freshets from Talla and Fruid reservoirs into the Tweed when required to maintain water quality downstream or to allow salmon access for spawning in the autumn. Some otherwise 'natural' rivers, such as Thurso and Helmsdale, have the facility to release water, via sluices, from lochs in the headwaters.

Initial river-level prospects for the 2019 fishing season were not good. In winter 2018/2019 much of Scotland received less than average rainfall. As a result Scotland began the summer of 2019 with lower reserves of water than at the same time last year but, after a dry spring, water levels improved.

Changing Water Temperature

Salmon is a cold-water species and needs strict temperature conditions to survive and thrive. River temperatures significantly affect the distribution, health, and survival of our salmon. Atlantic salmon exhibit thermal stress at temperatures above approximately 23 degrees C with mortality around 33 degrees C. Temperatures above 29°C can be lethal to juvenile salmon. River temperatures also affect salmon migration and taking behaviour for angling. Migration is judged to be affected at temperatures above 16 degrees C, with little movement from estuaries into rivers at the 20-23 degree C level.

Hot summers are a natural occurrence on some salmon rivers. The River Tweed Commissioner's Annual Report for 1976, a famously hot summer, reported temperatures as high as 27 degrees C in places on the main Tweed and tributaries in July and August. Water temperatures of 27°C and 25°C were recorded in Scotland in 2013 and 2014. Climate change projections suggest significant increases in global river temperatures before the end of the century, even under the more conservative scenario. Scottish rivers are thought to be particularly susceptible to such change, with an increase of 2°C or more predicted by 2050 for rivers in the Scottish Highlands. An increase of 2-3°C has already been observed on the River Spey over the last century.

The Scotland River Temperature Monitoring Network (SRTMN) was established in 2013 using temperature data-loggers (automatically recording temperature sensors) to provide data which has been used to produce models that can map those regions of the rivers which are most vulnerable to further temperature change. These data are available as online tools through the National Marine Plan Interactive (NMPi) website and have been used by a number of District Salmon Fishery Boards and Trusts to undertake extensive tree planting, particularly in head waters, to provide shade to reduce water temperatures. The rivers deemed to have the highest management priority as a result of predicted high river temperatures and high climate sensitivity are concentrated in the far north of Scotland in the areas of Sutherland, Ross and Cromarty and Inverness-shire.

Not all 'hot spots' are to be found in the headwaters. Marine Scotland Science has found significant 'hot spots' in the lower part of the Tweed. Additional shading is needed in these lower areas and these are the most difficult places to deal with. The Tweed is large and wide by this stage and so, even with landowner cooperation, additional planting might not make the substantial shading contribution that is required. Prime farmland in the lower stretches also presents difficulties, with farmers less inclined to give up land for tree planting. The issue is, of course, a complex one. Tree planting in the uplands may be useful for a number of other reasons but, in the Tweed catchment and for fish, it is the lowlands that need the temperature change.

As noted earlier, across the Atlantic, protecting cold-water refuges is a focus of conservation work on Canada's Miramichi river. This seen as a crucial adaptation strategy in the face of warming rivers. The Department of Fisheries and Oceans manages the river under a 'warm water protocol,' which protects adult fish that use cold pools on their way to spawn. If river temperatures climb above 20 degrees for 48 consecutive hours, the Department of Fisheries and Oceans closes 26 cold-water refuges to fishing to protect salmon from additional stress. If it gets hotter than 23 degrees, anglers are only allowed to fish in the morning. In 2018 the cold pools were shut down for nearly a month and a half, from July 5 to August 21.

Mitigating climate change - renewable energy from the rivers

Hydro-electricity is promoted as an effective way of reducing greenhouse gas emissions and mitigating the effect of climate change. Scotland's waters have been providing renewable energy at the Falls of Foyers on Loch Ness since 1895. The

North of Scotland Hydro-Electric Board developed 'Power from the Glens' in the 1940s and 1950s leading to the developments on the Tummel-Garry, Conon, Shin, Awe and Ness. The potential impacts of these projects on salmon rivers are well-known and the mitigation measures have been applied with varying degrees of success.

Small-scale hydro-electric power generation has been associated with fish-ladders on existing weirs - Blantyre on the Clyde, Philiphaugh on the Ettrick. A project on the South Esk at Kinnaird, uses the principle of an 'Archimedes Screw' to minimise damage to migrating smolts. Recent financial incentives have encouraged the development of 'run-of-river' projects, diverting river water through a turbine and back to the river without the need for an impoundment. The financial attraction of such schemes may impact our salmon rivers much more in the future and these impacts are uncertain.

CHAPTER 12

The Power Houses
Looking After The Watersheds

"Management efforts are now focused on reducing the impacts on salmon at all stages in the life cycle, particularly those in freshwater, these being direct, measurable and recognizing the imperative of sustaining healthy freshwater environments. The manager's tools now include preserving and restoring river habitat, minimizing and eliminating fish passage constraints, eliminating habitat fragmentation, and managing land use activities.

S. Rocque: Salmon Summit, 2011

The watersheds and the upper tributaries are usually considered to be the 'powerhouses' of the salmon system. Not only do they include the common spawning areas and the nursery areas for young fish but they also control the flow of water into our rivers and ultimately the opportunities for angling for salmon.   However, Ronald Campbell of the Tweed Foundation makes the point that :

"....the salmon looks like an upland species because it has survived best in such areas which have not had the development found in lowland areas. Actually, the salmon is as much a lowland species as an upland - and the best hope for salmon as a species today is the recovery of lowland rivers and their re-colonisation, for example, on the Mersey and Trent in the United Kingdom and the Seine, Elbe and Rhine in Europe.

The Tweed is largely a lowland river that has kept its salmon and has seen lowland tributaries like the Leader and Gala recover their populations. A lot of Tweed's spawning areas, for example, are not what we would consider 'upland': the whole of the lower Tweed is under 50m above sea level and the middle Tweed, under 100m.   Also, the Tweed catchment has not changed since the enormous rod catches we had in 2010 and 2011.   It could be argued that the best thing for the salmon, as a species, is the restoration of the lowland rivers to increase the number of populations and. ......there are now more salmon rivers than there have been for at least 100 years because of the recovery of these rivers!"

Previous chapters summarise the impacts of climate change on the quality, quantity and temperature of our salmon rivers. But there are some wider multi-disciplinary processes on the watersheds which can be directed towards making our rivers more fit for salmon and angling. To some extent the low rod-catches in 2018 were affected by low river levels. The low river-levels were affected, partly, by the inability of our watersheds to retain winter rainfall and release it gradually during the summer or by their tendency to release summer downpours too quickly to create short-lived spates. Much of this is controlled by the vegetation, drainage and land use in the watersheds.

Changing land-use in the watersheds.

The uplands of Scotland have traditionally supported a pastoral economy and been grazed by sheep and cattle. Many highland areas are also managed as deer forests and grazed by red deer. Many of the upland slopes have been virtually grazed naked and water runs rapidly off the slopes with little absorption and recharge to groundwater.

Sheep country in the Tweed catchment

In various forms, hill farming is the most widespread economic activity in the uplands, based upon sheep and cattle. Since 1999, and particularly since 2003, as a result in a change of European Union subsidies, there has been a general 'Retreat from the Hills" - as hill farming became uneconomic. Stock numbers have reduced, cattle have replaced sheep on some hillsides and other farms have been sold and converted to forestry. The reductions in livestock has resulted in changes to grazing patterns and changes in vegetation. With the loss of sheep, close-cropped upland sward has reverted to longer grassland. In time, longer grassland is colonised by gorse, bramble, birch and other scrub to create a diverse vegetation more capable of reducing surface runoff and flood risk - to the benefit of salmon rivers.

There is now an initiative known as "The Return to the Hills" based upon hill-farm diversification, the application of new technology and applied research with an emphasis on environmental sustainability, including woodland planting. This also has the potential to benefit salmon rivers.

"Slowing the Flow" - Natural Flood Management

Working with natural processes to manage the sources and pathways of flood waters can benefit flood risk in other parts of the catchment. Natural Flood Management (NFM) combines a number of related techniques and processes - all designed to "Slow the Flow" - reducing the rate at which rainwater reaches the rivers and causes spates and floods. The benefits and techniques of Natural Food Management are well-documented by World Wide Fund for Nature (WWF) and the Scottish Environment Protection Agency. Natural Flood Management should involve whole river ecosystems, from the blanket bogs of the watersheds to the floodplains of the lowlands. In the lower reaches projects include creating wetlands and sediment traps; restoring river meanders and floodplain processes and planting trees in the riparian zones. In the uplands, changes to land management and the restoration of natural habitats, such as peatlands, grasslands and woodlands create more space for water and helps reduce the flow of excess water to areas downstream.

The Scottish Environment Protection Agency has produced maps of 'Opportunity Areas for Runoff Reduction'. The amount of runoff that makes its way to rivers is influenced by many factors including the slope of the land, the extent to which the soils allow infiltration of water and the way the land is used. These are the areas which offer the best opportunities for holding back the rainfall before it reaches the rivers to cause flooding and also for storing water in the uplands to reduce the risk of drought. This could reduce the volatility of angling conditions and would become more important if rainfall patterns change as predicted. The greatest areas of such opportunities for 'run-off reduction' are in the west and north-west Highlands but other areas are identified in the Grampians, Cairngorms, Galloway and in the uplands around the Tweed catchment, particularly the Tweedsmuir Hills.

Tweed Forum

Tweed Forum is co-ordinating natural flood management measures across 60 sites in the Tweed river system, including the Ettrick and Yarrow valleys, upper Teviot, Gala Water, Bowmont Water and Eddleston Water. The aims of the projects are to slow the flow of surface water from headwaters, through controlling livestock grazing pressure; restoring natural river processes and by creating native woodland habitats. Three particular processes have the potential to benefit our salmon rivers: a) restoring rivers to a natural state; b) restoring peatland and c) creation woodland at a landscape scale.

Restoring rivers to a natural state

River restoration, involves the re-establishment of natural physical processes, features and habitats in rivers which have been destroyed. Terkel Broe Christensen, describes the restoration of Denmark's River Skjerne, the largest project of its kind in Northern Europe. The Skjerne is a lowland river which could produce multi-sea winter salmon up to 58lb in 1954. Subsequent obstruction, pollution and canalisation left the total salmon population estimated as low as 25 fish, with extinction forecast within a few years. A major restoration project through the 1990s removed dams, reduced pollution, restored the original meanders and created riffles and rapids with flow-deflectors. The restoration was completed in 2003 and by 2010, 1149 salmon were caught. Remaining optimism is so high that some enthusiasts are predicting an eventual run of 12,000-15,000 fish.

Professor Chris Spray, Dundee University, has been actively involved in the Eddleston Water Project. This tributary of the River Tweed at was straightened at the start of 19th century. The project aims to reduce the risk of flooding in Eddleston and Peebles by restoring some of the natural features of the catchment. This involves re-creating some of the river's previous meanders, planting over 200,000 trees and creating new wetlands.

The Forth Rivers Trust is running a 4-year RiverLife project which includes a major engineering project in the Bathgate Water in West Lothian. A tributary of the River Avon, the river has been 'lost' in historic and current urban and industrial development and downgraded due to straightening and over-widening. It currently has no invertebrates or fish life and resembles a ditch more than a river. It is, however, an important tributary of the River Avon and the restoration works will create a more sinuous and natural channel by restoring channel morphology, allowing life to return to the Bathgate Water.

Re-watering the Garry

Water had been abstracted from the River Garry for hydro-power since the 1950s. This had left approximately 21 km of the river with practically no flow and it duly lost its salmon population. However, prompted by the EU Water Framework Directive a restoration project was agreed in 2016, between Scottish and Southern Energy, Scottish Environment Protection Agency and the Tay District Salmon Fishery Board. An agreed flow was officially restored on 30 October 2017 and, by early November, adult salmon and approximately 30 redds were observed in the newly restored area. This should produce additional smolts for the Tummel-Garry part of the Tay system.

Restoring peatlands

Although the primary driver for peatland restoration is climate change, the process has considerable benefits for salmon and salmon rivers. Peatlands store vast amounts of carbon, which helps to mitigate climate change, and provide a unique habitat for wildlife. Blanket bogs are the 'sponges' of the hills. They absorb and store rainfall in winter and release it slowly in the summer, providing a more steady flow into the rivers.

Systematic drainage of upland peat bogs has been happening since the early nineteenth century. One old account describes the draining of peat bogs: 'which gradually flowed into burns and rivulets... the draining of these bogs has neither benefitted the sheep nor the salmon fishery'. Another observer records that, at Bridge of Allan in the Forth catchment: "Two hundred years ago the land in the upper reaches of the Allan was not drained, as it is today. The great spates we now have were consequently unknown then. The river did not rise so rapidly as it does today, and it never fell so low..." Damage to the peatlands has continued over subsequent years.

Scottish Natural Heritage published a National Peatland Plan in 2015 and established the PeatlandACTION Programme. This now provides some £18 million funding for peatland restoration usually in the form of blocking the old drainage ditches to reduce run-off and re-profiling the peat "hags" to reduce erosion. By 2019, almost 20,000 hectares of peatlands had been restored but many of Scotland's peatlands are still not in good condition.

The MoorsLIFE project in the Pennines of the north of England is one of the earliest examples. This was the biggest moorland conservation project in Europe and the results of this type of restoration on river management is compelling. Parts of the project demonstrated improvements to river regimes by:

- increasing the time for storm-flows to reach the rivers by up to 267%;
- by reducing peak storm discharge levels by up to 37% and
- smoothing the rise and fall of water levels by up to 38%.

Under the Scottish Natural Heritage PeatlandACTION Programme, a number of peatland restoration programmes have already been implemented throughout Scotland both in upland blanket bogs and lowland raised bogs. Butterfly Conservation (Scotland) runs a programme of volunteer 'Bog Squad' events to restore mainly lowland bogs and Buglife Scotland also carries out peatland restoration for biodiversity. Perhaps the largest and most notable example is the restoration of the vast blanket bogs of the Flow Country of Caithness and Sutherland where inappropriate plantations of Sitka spruce have been dug up to restore the peatland to a functioning ecosystem again. Regrettably, in 2019, a massive fire destroyed large areas of the dried-out peat before recovery could take place.

Diane Baum, Biologist with the Lochaber Fisheries Trust explains the potential benefits of peatland restoration for fisheries:

"For many years the freshwater fisheries sector has acknowledged the need for catchment-scale management policies that consider the condition of the wider physical and biological environment in order to improve fish populations. This is not only a more effective way of managing fish stocks, it also allows us to potentially find new partners and, crucially, to unlock new sources of funding. Scottish Natural Heritage's PeatlandACTION programme provides just such an opportunity for fishery managers and landowners. Peatland that is bare of vegetation and actively eroding can exacerbate extreme water flows and contribute to the sedimentation of our rivers. The result is a greater risk of redd washout, more pronounced droughts and the silting up of juvenile salmon and trout habitat."

Tweed Forum has restored blanket bogs in the Tweed catchment at Dryhope and Winterhope Moss in 2018. Further restoration works were carried out at Peel Fell, above Wauchope Forest and four further restoration projects include Gameshope valley, Carrifran, Grey Mare's Tail and Leadburn.

Peel Fell - Before restoration - Bare, eroded peat

Peel Fell - After restoration - 'Holding the water back'

Courtesy: Tweed Forum

At Peel Fell, funding, secured through the PeatlandACTION Programme, allowed for the restoration of a 10-hectare area of severely-eroded peat. Using brash-spreading techniques, large areas of bare mineral soil and peat-hags were re-vegetated. Gullied areas were blocked with bunds and 2800 m of peat-pans were re-profiled. All these projects will help to regulate the flows and should help to provide more stable river levels and better angling conditions in due course.

Planting trees at a landscape-scale - re-wilding the uplands

Although the primary driver for tree-planting is climate change, they also provide major benefits for salmon and salmon rivers. Trees are the 'lungs' of the uplands. They produce oxygen and absorb carbon dioxide. Planting trees is now widely recognised as an effective means of mitigating climate change. For each new hectare of forest and woodland created, it is estimated that, on average, seven tonnes of CO_2 will be removed from the atmosphere each year. In 2016, around 12 million tonnes of CO_2 was removed. While carbon capture is seen to be one of the main drivers for woodland expansion, forest and woodland also have an important role in natural flood management - provided the 'right tree' is planted in the 'right place' - for helping to regulate salmon rivers.

Planting woodlands on a landscape-scale can potentially have a great effect on the rate at which rainwater passes into the river. Well-sited woodlands can slow peak flows and reduce flood peaks downstream. At the same time they can reduce erosion and the amount of silt entering watercourses. They can reduce water yield by improving the infiltration rates of woodland soils and by 'sponging up' water through the process of evapotranspiration. A 10% increase in conifer or broad-leaved forest cover within a catchment could achieve a 40mm and 25mm decrease in water yield, respectively. There has to be a balance here. While this might reduce flood risk in wet weather, it might not be so helpful under drought conditions when the rivers are desperate for water?

In the last 100 years, Scotland's forest cover has increased from around 5% of the country's land cover to 18.5% in 2018. The industrial, intensive, single-purpose forestry, usually of Sitka spruce, that dominated from 1960s to the early 1980s, has been replaced by an approach which takes account of wider environmental and social interests and aim towards multi-purpose forests. This is reflected in the Forestry and Land Management (Scotland) Act 2018 and the associated Scotland's Forestry Strategy, 2019–2029. In September 2019, the Scottish Government announced new targets for planting 12,000 ha in 2020 and 15,000 ha by 2025. This will be funded by an additional £5 million investment to support its contribution to tackling climate change.

Native woodland initiatives

A number of initiatives are increasing Scotland's cover of native woodlands, with all their benefits for landscape, biodiversity and recreation. They also benefit salmon rivers by regulating floods, water temperature and by providing nutrients and food.

Loch Garry Tree Group. This pioneering group was established by freshwater biologist, Ron Greer, in 1974. On the bare hillsides and shores of Loch Garry, near Dalnaspidal, Ron planted native trees to provide leaf-litter food and nutrients for the population of Arctic charr in the loch. Rowan, willow, alder, hawthorn, sessile oak, birch, elm, holly, gean and Scots pine were all planted - at an unusually high altitude of 1400 ft (470 m) above sea level.

Other landscape-scale native woodland initiatives, which can benefit rivers, include *Trees for Life,* a charity which focusses on re-wilding the Scottish Highlands. *Woodland Trust Scotland (WTS)* manages and some 60 woods from Sutherland to Stranraer. Since 2000, the Trust has been *"Re-wilding Glen Devon"* by planting around 1.5 million trees to re-create native woodland, on a substantial area of previous sheep-runs in the Ochil Hills.

"Re-wilding Glen Devon" - Native woodland planting in the Forth catchment

The Borders Forest Trust has planted over 1.5 million native trees in the Borders and Dumfriesshire since 1996 and expects to exceed 2 million by 2020. It has a particular concentration in the Tweedsmuir Hills with Carrifran Wildwood, Corehead Farm and the Devil's Beef Tub and the Talla and Gameshope estate reviving the *Wild Heart of Southern Scotland*.

The *South Esk Catchment Management Partnership* has operated a 'Contour Planting Project' in Glen Clova since 2015 to improve natural flood management, control diffuse pollution, and to improve the local landscape and habitats. The increase in woodland cover should lead to an improvement in water quality and, in the long term, a reduction in the peak water level during flood events.

At *Jerah,* Scotland's largest new forest was planted in 2015 on a 1,000-ha former sheep farm in the Ochil Hills. With 1.3 million trees of 16 different species this new Jerah Forest is designed, not only to produce a productive timber crop, but also to create amenity woodland and sequester 183,000 tonnes of

CO2 in its 40-year rotation. A research project at Heriot-Watt University is assessing the new forest's contribution to natural flood management in Menstrie glen.

Mitigating climate change - renewable energy from the uplands

On-shore wind farms are also promoted as a source of renewable energy. For all their benefits in reducing greenhouse gas emissions, they too can have impacts on salmon rivers. Fish populations can be affected by a deterioration in water quality caused by sediment, fuel and concrete spillage, tree-felling during construction all of which can have an effect on spawning success and juvenile salmon. Other challenges include obstructions to fish migration by poorly-designed culverts and alterations to surface runoff and drainage. The risks of such impacts have to be reduced by careful planning and good practice throughout construction.

Reality Check

A long-term study of salmon and sea trout in the Burrishoole system in Ireland, published in 2016, confirmed the role that an ecosystem approach, using long-term ecological monitoring, must play in providing the evidence needed to manage salmon and sea trout stocks. This study noted that salmon and sea trout are at risk in marine, transitional, and freshwater environments, as well as the overarching impact of climate change. However, any relationship with land-use change paled into insignificance in comparison with some direct anthropogenic impacts. In the Burishoole system this included the stocking of hatchery-reared salmon and the reduced marine survival caused by sea-lice.

CHAPTER 13

Salmon in a Joined-up World
Collaborating for our Salmon

"The big picture going forward will be that we need to be proactive in ensuring that the salmon's interests are represented in long-term planning and we need to focus on the entire ecosystem; habitat improvements aimed at the salmon should bring benefits for other diadromous species that may, in turn, assist salmon stocks to re-build. Coupling our interests with those of the diadromous species complex will not only allow us to take a broader ecosystem level view, but it may make a larger pool of resources available to us.

Timothy F Sheehan: *Salmon Summit,* 2011

There is no doubt that Scotland's salmon are having to adapt to a changing climate, both in the freshwater environment and in the oceans. Any management action we can exert directly is mainly in the freshwater environment. Although there may appear to be an 'adequate' number of smolts being produced, a more integrated management of our watersheds might improve the river environment to ensure that as many smolts as possible make it down the river to the sea. While the priority has to be making the downstream smolt migration as safe as possible the management of the watersheds might provide a safer river highway. This is where some more joined-up thinking may add value.

The watersheds - the need for joined-up thinking

Although there is already some 'connectivity' between rural land-use and fisheries, a much more integrated and 'connected' approach may be required. Upland catchments have a large number of stakeholders and are subject to a wide range of sectoral strategies and programmes. In addition to the management decisions of individual landowners, upland catchments are subject to a number of strategies which do not always match up or take account of salmon or salmon fishing interests. Some relevant strategies and programmes are:

- Scottish Planning Policy (Scottish Government);
- Local Development Plans and associated Supplementary Guidance (Local Authority);
- Flood risk management plans (Scottish Environment Protection Agency/Local authorities);
- Forest and Woodland Strategies (Local Authority/Forestry Scotland);
- Biodiversity Action Plans (Local Authority/Scottish Natural Heritage);
- Hill farming (Scottish Rural Development Programme);
- Peatland restoration (Scottish Natural Heritage, Peatland Action);

- Land drainage (Scottish Rural Development Programme)/ Scottish Environment Protection Agency);
- Flood risk management (Scottish Environment Protection Agency/Local authorities);
- Forestry (Forestry Scotland);
- Native woodland planting (Forestry Scotland)
- District Salmon Fishery Boards and River and Fisheries Trusts;

The lack of joined-up policy-making was highlighted by Professor Sarah Skerrat, Director of Rural Policy at the Scottish Rural Colleges. Speaking at the annual Spring conference of Scottish Land and Estates on 15 May 2019 she complained that "policy tended to operate in parallel rather than in a cohesive manner." She decried the lack of 'connectivity' between the various Scottish land-use policies and initiatives over recent years. "These often conclude leaving tensions unresolved and opportunities not realised."

Climate change, population growth, economics, and environmental legislation all necessitate a move towards a more integrated, catchment-based approach to the management of land and water. Working in this way creates efficiencies in managing the environment by recognising that many issues in catchments affect many different sectors. Where land and water are managed together at the catchment scale this can bring about whole catchment improvements and multiple benefits. If the upland catchments can be managed as an integrated ecosystem, perhaps the salmon resource, within the freshwater environment, might be maximised.

Scottish Government Directorates

'Joined-up thinking' has to start at the top. The Scottish Government has a number of Directorates, each with some influence on the issues affecting the Atlantic salmon.

• *Environment and Forestry Directorate* is responsible for Scottish Environment Protection Agency and Scottish Natural Heritage - both of whom are integral to salmon and salmon rivers.

• *Marine Scotland Directorate* works closely with Scottish Natural Heritage and the Scottish Environment Protection Agency to ensure, as far as salmon are concerned, the sustainable management of freshwater fish and fisheries resources, fisheries regulations, promoting sustainable, profitable and well-managed fisheries and aquaculture industries and ensuring a sound scientific evidence base.

• *Agriculture and Rural Economy Directorate* is responsible for agricultural policy and rural land management - which have an impact on salmon rivers.

• *Energy and Climate Change Directorate* promotes Scotland's climate change, clean energy and energy efficiency programmes and supervises the water industry - aspects which affect salmon rivers.

• *Local Government and Communities Directorate* responsible for statutory planning - which has an indirect effect on salmon rivers.

• *Culture, Tourism and Major Events Directorate's* purpose is to build Scotland's influence and reputation abroad - which should include salmon fishing.

No doubt to encourage some 'joined-up' thinking, an *Environment and Economy Leaders' Group* (EELG) is designed to bring together the family of environment and other land-based public bodies with Scottish Government Directors.

There are still perceived 'disconnects' between the welfare of wild salmon and a number of issues - fish-farming; forestry; predation; recreational access; introduced species eg beaver;

aspects of natural flood management and renewable energy. These are still to be resolved.

River basin management plans

River basin management planning requires co-ordination and integration, working in partnership. The Scottish Environment Protection Agency operates a number of multi-stakeholder groups including a National Advisory Group and eleven Area Advisory Groups, which might have 26 members. A Fish and Fisheries Advisory Group is made up of representatives from responsible authorities, national stakeholders and organisations working on fisheries at a strategic level. It provides fisheries advice and information to protect fish populations and fisheries interests and ensure that they are taken into account in the River Basin Management Plan process. At present it includes representatives from:

- Fisheries Management Scotland,
- Scottish Government, Marine Scotland,
- Scottish Government, Water Environment Policy,
- Scottish Natural Heritage,
- Environment Agency (cross-Border corresponding member),
- The academic sector.

Catchment Management

At a river-catchment level, there are already some good examples of integrated catchment management - e.g. Tweed Forum, the River South Esk Catchment Partnership and all Rivers and Fisheries Trusts are committed to this concept through their Fisheries Management Plans. But much more could be done to support these initiatives to enhance the salmon rivers.

Tweed Forum was formed in 1991 - pre-dating the EU Water Framework Directive - to "promote the sustainable use of the whole of the Tweed catchment through holistic and integrated management and planning". Members from both sides of the Border ensures that the whole of the Tweed catchment is looked after. One of the main lessons learned is that working in a loose but focused partnership has enabled the design and delivery of a range of habitat restoration projects. Without a partnership these projects would not have been possible.

The River Spey Catchment Management Plan was first launched in 2003 and last reviewed in November 2016. The Executive Summary expresses the value of the process:

> "Catchment Management Planning has become an established mechanism for developing a cohesive and holistic approach to large scale stewardship of the water environment. For the Spey catchment it offers a way of collating and summarising in one document the key issues, pressures and opportunities as they pertain to a geographic area as defined by the river network. By recognising the links between the health of a river and associated land use, it aims to enable all those with an interest in the river to communicate, liaise and work more effectively together."

The River South Esk Catchment Partnership was formed in 2004 when ongoing pressures on the river reinforced the·need to develop a more joined-up approach to the way the water resource was managed. A Catchment Management Plan was prepared in 2008 which set out a framework, which helps protect and improve the quality of the water, wildlife and local area.

The *River Dee Trust* recognises that its work in improving upland stream habitat needs to be carried out on a catchment scale. With the continued support of the estates on upper Deeside they continue to create riparian woodland and to involve volunteers from the local communities. The Trust has built up strong relationships with land managers in the upper Dee catchment, as the salmon fishery on Deeside has an important cultural and economic role to play. Working closely with keepers, shepherds and land managers they have designed all riparian tree planting to maximise benefits for salmon, without negatively impacting the movement of deer or disrupting traditional grouse drives.

The *Forth Fisheries Trust* has a different take on catchment management - emphasising the importance of people. Alison Baker, Director of the Trust, writes:

> "An obvious, but often forgotten, point in the world of fisheries management is that we cannot manage the fishery without managing the river, we cannot manage the river without managing the land and we cannot manage the land without active interaction with the people who use the land."

This approach is at the heart of a new project being undertaken by the Trust called: *RiverLife: Almond and Avon*. Damage to the rivers caused by human intervention over 300 years includes constructing barriers to fish passage, straightening channels and dredging. The vision of the *RiverLife* project – to reconnect wildlife and communities to their local rivers – may seem a world away from fisheries management. But, while firmly based on the need to improve the environment for freshwater fish, the project will provide the basis for a better understanding of the interlinks between all wildlife living on, and in, the rivers and also how the rivers can interact positively with those living near them.

Regional Land Use Partnerships

In 2016, the Scottish Government's *Second Land Use Strategy 2016-2021* (LUS2) promoted Regional Land Use Frameworks and Regional Land Use Partnerships as a mechanism to encourage a more integrated approach to land use. These had some promising features for watershed management. At the same time Scottish Natural Heritage was tasked to consult on views about *"A Strategic Vision for the Uplands"*. All went quiet for a few years until, in 2019, the Scottish Government's programme for 2019/2020 included an intention to:

> "…….make regional land use plans for maximising the potential of every part of Scotland's land to contribute to the fight against climate change. To do this, we will develop proposals for implementing regional partnerships and frameworks. Based on these proposals, we will work to enable regional land use partnerships to emerge locally by 2021. Each partnership will be tasked with creating a regional land use framework by 2023 that identifies where resource can have the biggest climate impact.

It will be important that Scotland's salmon have a voice in these partnerships and frameworks.

CHAPTER 14

A Surviving Species?
Prospects for the Future

".......Managers will also need to determine whether it is likely to be practical (or even possible) to maintain favourable environments for salmon in specific areas in the face of major climatic changes and engage with stakeholders in developing procedures for deciding when protection and restoration is no longer tenable."

E. C. E. Potter. *Salmon Summit,* 2011

In 1969, an American professor - Anthony Netboy - published *"The Atlantic Salmon - A Vanishing Species"*. Netboy described the human-induced causes of the salmon's decline from Portugal, Spain and France on the east side of the Atlantic and its demise from New England in the west - in the years before climate change was 'the elephant in the room'.

The Atlantic salmon is a cold water species. As the Quaternary ice-sheet shrank northwards, so the salmon followed, reducing or abandoning its southern part of its previous range. This may be a continuing process, bearing in mind the evidence of high salmon abundance in Arctic Russia over recent years.

In Canada, Ben Goldfarb describes Atlantic salmon turning up 400 kilometres north of the Arctic Circle in the Clyde River on Baffin Island. "If Atlantic salmon are indeed infiltrating the Canadian Arctic in greater numbers, there's an obvious potential culprit: climate change." says Goldfarb. "Our planet's oceans have absorbed more than 90 percent of the excess heat generated by global warming, driving many species poleward toward cooler climes."

Goldfarb believes it is a virtual certainty that *Salmo salar* will ultimately suffer. In southern New England, at the thermal limits of Atlantic salmon's range, fisheries managers have implicated climate change in the failure of runs to recover on rivers like the Farmington and the Connecticut. In Europe, models suggest that salmon could disappear from river basins throughout Portugal, Spain, and much of France by 2100.

In 2017 a report by the International Council on the Exploration of the Sea concluded. "It is extremely unlikely that Atlantic salmon as a species will become globally extinct within the next 100 years", as a result of climate change. "However, it is very likely that some populations will suffer significant reductions in abundance." Localized disappearance is neither as permanent nor quite as devastating as utter extinction. But for communities at the southern bounds of Atlantic salmon's range, the losses will feel no less final. In Scotland, the Atlantic salmon is a mainstay of some rural economies.

E. C. E. Potter in his paper on *Managing salmon stocks and fisheries in a changing environment* suggests that:

"Over recent decades, there have been marked changes in the patterns of growth and mortality of Atlantic salmon (Salmo salar) during both the freshwater and marine phases of their lifecycle and consequent effects on the structure and status of populations. In some cases, these changes have been due to factors that are within our control and can be alleviated by appropriate management action. Taking such action should clearly be given a high priority. However in other circumstances, such as modifications to the marine environment caused by climate change, there may not only be little that can be done to reverse the pressures but the severity of the impacts may also be expected to increase in the future. These changes, along with our management responses, will have implications for the optimal life-history strategies of the fish and thus how populations change. As a result, maintaining current management approaches, which generally involve trying to restore historic stock structures, may no longer be appropriate.

There is therefore a need to determine how managers should both plan for and respond to these changes in relation to the protection and restoration of stocks and the management of fisheries. Methods are required to forecast the likely impacts on habitats and the consequent effects on stocks in order that the best ameliorative actions can be taken at an early stage. Managers will also need to determine whether it is likely to be practical (or even possible) to maintain favourable environments for salmon in specific areas in the face of major climatic changes and engage with stakeholders in developing procedures for deciding when protection and restoration is no longer tenable."

Goldfarb is cautiously optimistic, however, for the survival of the species. If there is long-term hope for *Salmo salar*, it lies in the salmon's own proven tenacity in the face of environmental changes. The species has already overcome the fluctuation between an ice-age and a successive era of global warming. "Only time will tell," says Goldfarb, "but in the meantime it is essential to understand the extent of the salmon's northern range extension and identify and protect areas with cold springs and shaded streams. As the Arctic becomes more habitable, human interventions to preserve and enhance cold-water refuges may yet allow Atlantic salmon to survive and, perhaps, thrive again one day. Now that would be cool."

On another positive note, in Scotland, there are reports suggesting that there is no immediate cause for concern arising from the local juvenile surveys undertaken during the year. A number of rivers reported good numbers of fish within the spawning tributaries and on the redds at the end of the year. The results of the National Electrofishing Programme provides further information on the strength of juvenile fish numbers.

It is accepted that salmon stocks are cyclical both in their abundance and their composition. Historical data show swings from one-sea winter grilse to multi-sea winter salmon associated with the North Atlantic Multi-decadal Oscillation. The present low rod-catches appear to be related to a cyclical 'ebb' in the combined returns of grilse and salmon. Ronald Campbell illustrates with historical netting records between 1742-2018.

This phenomenon was observed by Tony George in 1990:

" The history of the Scottish salmon fishery over a long period of time shows that whenever a salmon period declines and a grilse period comes in there are, for a period of years, strong joint runs of both salmon and grilse in many large rivers (e.g. 1812-17; 1881-84; 1957-66) ....but when a grilse period declines and a salmon period comes in there is always a significant, albeit variable, gap in years before the salmon becomes established (e.g. 1780-92; 1850-5; 1897-1920).

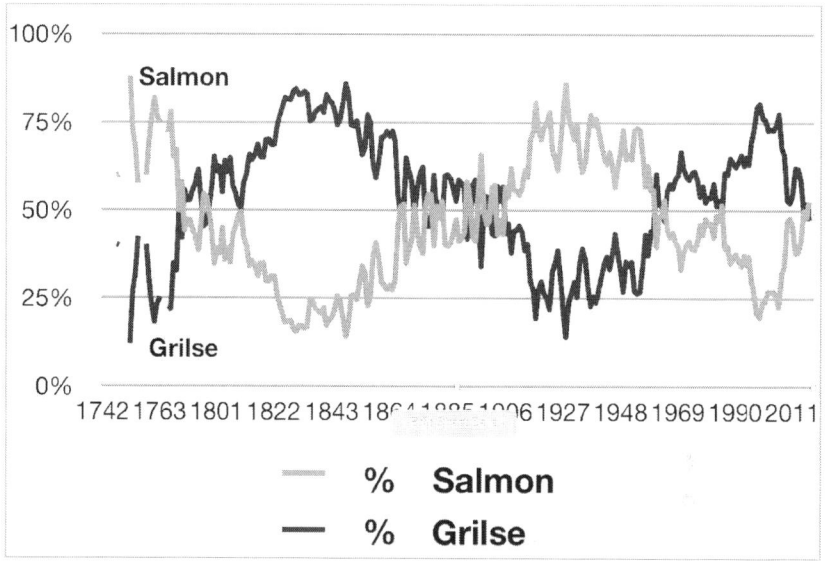

Tweed netting records 1742-2018 (smoothed x 3)
Fluctuations correlate with temperatures in the Arctic: (Warmer - salmon phase, Colder - grilse phase)

The Tweed Foundation

"During such periods, the fishery as a whole is at a low ebb and we are in just such a period now," Campbell suggests, "and we should expect the fishery to be at a 'low ebb.' Campbell guesses that, "As Arctic temperatures increase, we will get "stuck" in a warm period and so "stuck" in a salmon period with consequently lower numbers." Catch figures available for English rod-fisheries indicate that the present decline is very much a grilse decline and "was predictable". Campbell adds: "Given that we are going into a warmer Arctic phase. Multi-sea winter salmon catches seem to be holding up but we may have to give up on grilse as an important stock component".

2019 - Encouraging

The Tweed rod-catch in 2019 is encouraging. Fay Hieatt, Managing Director of the Tweed Foundation and Clerk to the River Tweed Commissioners, reports that,

"…..June's catch was the highest we've recorded for that month over the last five years. With May also seeing an improvement in catches which also topped that month's five-year average.   Spring fishing was better in 2019, particularly in the Lower Tweed." It was also noted that "Angling conditions were much more conducive to fishing for a large part of this season. There was enough rain to keep things relatively fresh, although proper flood conditions didn't arrive until early summer."

Looking to the future, Hieatt concludes, on a bright note, that:

"Whilst numbers of adult Salmon returning to the river are still low in Tweed angling terms ……. evidence from our electro-fishing surveys and fish counters shows that we still have enough fish to seed the next generation. This is the basis for the continuation of our salmon population. By protecting our juvenile stocks and by ensuring that as many smolts as possible then migrate safely to sea, we are giving our salmon the potential to return in greater numbers in future seasons."

But …… if the Greenland ice sheet continues to melt at its present rate there is a large and increasing volume of cold, fresh water adding to the North Atlantic feeding grounds.   With possible changes to salinity, temperatures and currents in the 'conveyor belt domain' the changes to the salmon's food chain, migrations and hence survival in the North Atlantic are unpredictable.

The Scottish Government's promised "multi-year national wild Atlantic salmon strategy" has a lot to cover before September 2020.

Selected References

Ashley, Kate. 2019: *Wild Salmon*. SPICe Briefing for Scottish Parliament, 19 August 2019. Edinburgh.

Atlantic Salmon Trust. 2019. *Atlantic salmon mortality at sea: Developing an evidence-based "Likely Suspects" Framework*. Based on a workshop organised by the Atlantic Salmon Trust, held in Edinburgh Tuesday, 6th November – 8th November 2017.

Barnett, C. et al. *Handbook of climate trends across Scotland*. Sniffer Project CC03, Scotland and Northern Ireland Forum for Environmental Research.

Baum, D. 2018. *Peatland restoration: how rivers can reap the rewards*. Fisheries Management Scotland, Annual Review, 2018. Edinburgh.

Campbell, Dr R. 2017/2018. *Annual Reports 2017 and 2018*. (and pers. comms.) The Tweed Foundation. Drygrange. Melrose.

Christensen, Terkel Broe. 2019. *The Ugly Duckling*. Atlantic Salmon Journal, Summer 2019.

Davidson, B. 2019. *2018: A Year of Extremes*. Fisheries Management Scotland, Annual Review, 2019. Edinburgh.

Eddleston Water Project. (undated). *Leaflet-The-Eddleston-Water-Project.pdf*. Tweed Forum.

European Union. 2009. *Conservation of Atlantic Salmon in Scotland*. CASS Project Number LIFE04NAT/GB/000250. ec,europa.eu.environment.

Eyto, E. et al. 2016. *The response of North Atlantic diadromous fish to multiple stressors, including land use change: a multidecadal study*. Can. J. Fish. Aquat. Sci. 73: 1–11.

George, A.F. 1982. *Cyclical Variations in the Return Migration of Scottish Salmon by Sea-Age c.1790 to 1976.* MPhil thesis. The Open University.

Goldfarb, Ben. 2019. *Too Hot to Handle? Salmon and Climate.* Atlantic Salmon Journal, Summer 2019.

Harrison, J. G. 2012. *The Eddleston Water - Historical Change in Context.* A Report for the Tweed Forum. Melrose.

ICES Journal of Marine Science. 2012. *International Symposium on Salmon at Sea: Scientific Advances and their Implications for Management.* Volume 69, Issue 9, November 2012.

Kendon, et. al. 2019. *State of the UK Climate 2018.* International Journal of Climatology Vol 39 Issue S1. Royal Meteorological Society, London.

Knight, P. 2011. *Chairman's Summary - Implications for Salmon Management.* International Atlantic Salmon Research Board. Salmon Summit 2011.

Knight, R. 2019. *Predation of Atlantic salmon.* Fisheries Management Scotland, Annual Review, 2019. Edinburgh.

Mckelvey, S. 2018. *Nutrient enhancement – a new strategy to improve juvenile production.* Fisheries Management Scotland, Annual Review, 2018. Edinburgh.

North Atlantic Salmon Conservation Organisation (NASCO) and International Atlantic Salmon Research Board. *Salmon Summit 2011.* Edinburgh.

Pilkington, M. et al. 2015. *Restoration of Blanket bogs; flood risk reduction and other ecosystem benefits,* Final report of the Making Space for Water project: Moors for the Future Partnership. Edale.

Potter, E.C.E. 2011. *Managing salmon stocks and fisheries in a changing environment.* International Atlantic Salmon Research Board. Salmon Summit 2011. Abstracts.

Purseglove,. J. 2017. *Taming the Flood.* (Third Edition), Harper Collins, London.

River Dee Trust, 2018. *Smolt migration through the River Dee and Harbour.* January 2018. (and update on website 2019)

Rocque, S. 2011.*What tools are left in the manager's toolbox – challenges to conservation of Atlantic salmon in eastern Canada.* International Atlantic Salmon Research Board. Salmon Summit 2011.

Russell, I. et al.2011. *The influence of the freshwater environment and the biological characteristics of Atlantic salmon smolts on their subsequent marine survival.* International Atlantic Salmon Research Board. Salmon Summit 2011.

Scotland River Temperature Monitoring Network (SRTMN) *Predictions of river temperature and sensitivity to climate change.*

Scottish Environment Protection Agency. 2011. *Flood Risk Management Strategies and Local Flood Risk Management.* Stirling.

Scottish Environment Protection Agency. 2013. *Identifying Opportunities for Natural Flood Management.* Stirling.

Scottish Environment Protection Agency. 2015. *Natural Flood Management Handbook.* Stirling.

Scottish Environment Protection Agency. 2015. *Opportunity Areas for Runoff Reduction.* Stirling.

Scottish Environment Protection Agency. 2015 *The River Basin Management Plan for the Scotland River Basin District 2015–2020 Summary.* Stirling.

Scott-Dempster. R. 2019. *Will tighter regulation pave the way for closed containment salmon farming?*. Fisheries Management Scotland, Annual Review, 2019. Edinburgh.

Scottish Government. 2010. *Low Carbon Scotland: Meeting the Emissions Reduction Targets 2010-2022*. Edinburgh.

Scottish Government. 2011 *Delivering Sustainable Flood Risk Management*. Edinburgh.

Scottish Government. 2016 *Getting the best from our land -a Land Use Strategy for Scotland 2016 - 2021*.Edinburgh.

Scottish Government, Marine Science. 2018. *Where Should We Plant Trees To Protect Rivers From High Water Temperatures?* Topic Sheet Number 91 V2.

Scottish Government. 2019. *Protecting Scotland's Future: the Government's programme for Scotland 2019-2020*. September 2019. Edinburgh.

Scottish Natural Heritage. 2014. *Scotland's National Peatland Plan,* Inverness.

Scottish Parliament. 2019. Motion S5M-15657. *"Long-term Decline in Salmon Stocks"*. 4 April 2019. Edinburgh.

Sheehan. T.F. 2011. *Take Home Message by Timothy F Sheehan, NOAA Fisheries, USA.* International Atlantic Salmon Research Board. Salmon Summit 2011.

Summers. D. 2018. *Restoring the River Garry.* Fisheries Management Scotland, Annual Review, 2018. Edinburgh.

Third. E. 2019. *'Habitat restoration on the upper Dee'.* Fisheries Management Scotland, Annual Review, 2019. Edinburgh.

Wells. Dr. A. 2019. *Fish farming – time to deliver.* Fisheries Management Scotland, Annual Review, 2019. Edinburgh.

World Wide Fund for Nature (WWF). Undated. *Flood Planner. A Manual for the Natural Management of River Floods.* Dunkeld.

NERC. 2018. *National River Flow Archive, 2018,* Centre for Ecology and Hydrology, Wallingford.

Whelan. K. 2011. *The SALSEA Programme – unraveling the life of the Atlantic salmon at sea* and *Take Home Message.* International Atlantic Salmon Research Board. Salmon Summit 2011.

Windsor M.L. et al. 2012. *Atlantic salmon at sea: Findings from recent research and their implications for management.* NASCO document CNL(12)60. Edinburgh.

Wright. R. 2018/2019. *River Reports - Naver 2017 and 2018.* Fisheries Management Scotland, Annual Review, 2018 and 2019. Edinburgh.

Useful websites and links

Atlantic Salmon Trust (AST) *https://atlanticsalmontrust.org*

Fisheries Management Scotland (FMS) *http://fms.scot*

Marine Scotland Science (MMS): *https://www2.gov.scot/Topics/marine/Salmon-Trout-Coarse*

North Atlantic Salmon Conservation Organisation (NASCO). Salmon Summit 2011: http://www.nasco.int/sas/salmonsummit.htm. and further information at https://doi.org/10.1093/icesjms/fss013

Scottish Environment Protection Agency (SEPA) *https://www.sepa.org.uk*

Scottish Natural Heritage (SNH) *https://www.nature.scot*

Tweed Forum. *https://tweedforum.org*

The Tweed Foundation. *https://www.tweedfoundation.org.uk*

About The Author

Neil R Jamieson

Drew Jamieson is a geographer, angler, conservationist and writer. who has spent much of his career in fisheries and environmental planning. A Fellow of the Institute of Fisheries Management, he has researched, followed and commented upon the management and conservation of Scottish game fisheries for the past 50 years. At various times he has served on government committees and the Scottish Angler's National Association (SANA). He was the angling reporter for *The Scotsman* newspaper for many years and has contributed to many magazines including *Trout and Salmon, Fly Fishing and Fly Tying, Scottish Field* and the *Atlantic Salmon Journal.*

email: dumyat2@btinternet.com

Printed in Great Britain
by Amazon